GLOBAL WARMING

GLOBAL WARMING

Dr. K. S. Jauhari
M.A., NET/IRF, Ph.D.
Principal
Govt. Degree College,
Pankhal

The Readers Paradise
New Delhi - 110002

Global Warming

ISBN - 978-93-85958-80-9

Published by

THE READERS PARADISE

103, 4787/23, Ansari Road, Daryaganj,
New Delhi - 110002
011-23246222, 9811197091, 9312220441
thereadersparadisesales@gmail.com

Printed in India
Balaji Offset

CONTENTS

PREFACE

Global warming is one of the complex problems facing mankind today. This is evident from observations of increases in the global average air and ocean temperatures, widespread melting of snow and ice, and the rising global average sea level. It poses a variety of challenges with wide-ranging effects. It is projected to have significant impacts on conditions affecting agriculture, including temperature, precipitation and glacial run-off. Agriculture is the mainstay of the Indian economy and provides food and livelihood security to a substantial section of our population. Agriculture will be adversely affected not only by an increase or decrease in the overall amounts of rainfall but also by shifts in the timing of the rainfall. Any change in rainfall patterns poses a serious threat to agriculture, and therefore to the economy and food security. Rise in temperatures caused by increasing greenhouse gases is likely to affect crops differently from region to region. Erosion, submergence of shorelines, and salinity of the water-table due to the increased sea levels are the factors that mainly affect agriculture through inundation of low-lying areas. Increased frequencies of drought, floods, storms and cyclones are likely to increase the variability of agricultural production.

Lack of access to water is a matter of concern contributing to heightened competitions within the country. As the population expands and the consumption of water spirals upwards, water problems are bound to intensify. Increase in temperature due to climate change has been widespread over the globe. Global warming has resulted in decline in mountain glaciers and snow cover in both hemispheres and this is projected to accelerate throughout the 21st century. This will in turn lead to reducing water availability, hydropower potential, and would change the seasonal flow of rivers. Increasing flood pose challenges to society, physical infrastructure and water quality. Rising temperatures will further affect the physical, chemical and biological properties of fresh water lakes and rivers, with predominantly adverse impacts on marine life forms. The growing demand of water in agriculture, industrial and domestic sectors has brought problems of over-exploitation of the groundwater resource to the fore. The rise of the sea level under warming is inevitable. The coastal areas of our country face a grave risk from the sea level rise, which could flood land and cause damage to coastal infrastructure and other properties. Flooding will displace a large number of people from the coasts putting greater pressure on the civic amenities and rapid urbanisation. Climate change has the potential to cause immense biodiversity loss, affecting both individual species and their ecosystems that support economic growth and human well-being. Devastating effects on the native habitats of many animals and plants due to global warming is likely to drive a considerable number of today's known animal and plant species to extinction. Mountain ecosystems are hot-spots of biodiversity. However, temperature increases and human activities are causing fragmentation and degradation of mountain biodiversity. Climate change poses a host of threats to the survival of mankind. Emissions of the Green House Gases have been responsible for the depletion of the ozone layer, which protects the earth from harmful direct rays of the sun. Depletion of stratospheric ozone results in higher exposure to the ultra-violet rays of the sun, leading to an increase in the incidents of skin cancer. It is anticipated that there will be an increase in the number of deaths due to greater frequency and severity of heat waves and other extreme weather events. Climate change and the resulting higher global temperatures are causing increasing frequency of floods and droughts leading to the risk of disease infections.

India had adopted the National Environment Policy 2006 which provides for several measures and policy initiatives to create awareness about climate change and help capacity building for taking adaptation measures. On June 30, 2008 India unveiled its National Action Plan on Climate Change with a view to lay down the priorities and future actions of the government for addressing climate change and updating India's national programme relevant to addressing climate change. Eight national missions (solar mission, energy efficiency, sustainable habitat, water, Himalayan eco-system, Green India, eco-green agriculture and knowledge) have been specifically outlined to simultaneously advance India's development and climate change-related objectives of adaptation and GHG mitigation. India is committed to a path of sustainable development. To effectively address the concerns of climate change and to follow the path of sustainable development, the global energy diet, which is fossil fuels centric, must be changed. Efforts must be made to harness the potential of alternative sources of energy, such as hydro-power, solar and wind and progressively make transition to clean energy. The possibility of harnessing nuclear energy can also be explored for meeting the long-term energy needs. Investment in renewable energy infrastructure is a priority area for action.

India has taken several steps in the implementation of Clean Development Mechanism projects in the country. The idea of "national water grid" was scientifically studied by the Central Water Commission through the National Water Development Agency, an autonomous body under the Water Resources Ministry. The feasibility of using electricity and battery-operated vehicles is also being explored. Efforts are being made to extract energy from urban and industrial waste. The use of cheap plastic bags should be substituted with eco-friendly plastics. In areas of water scarcity, drought-proofing measures through water storage and rainwater harvesting can be applied.

Similarly, techniques to clean the fumes and smokes in cars and other vehicles should be introduced. Afforestation, preventing the felling of immature and young tress, and creating awareness amongst the local people about the importance of forests may help in conserving biological diversity. Recycling of fossil fuels can be the safest way to ensure conservation of minerals. The role of environmentalists, especially the non-governmental organisations, is very crucial in formulating effective policies for tackling climate change. Movements like the Chipko Andolan of 1976 bear testimony to the fact that the people of India are concerned about their habitat. Besides, R&D in alternative fuels and low carbon infrastructure must get due priority. Unless we develop indigenous green technology, we cannot attain sustainable development.

Global warming is the defining issue of our times. It should be addressed by all countries with a shared perspective, free from narrow and myopic considerations. We urgently need a new economic paradigm, which is global, inclusive, cooperative, environmentally sensitive and, above all, scientific. Sustainable development based on addressing the needs of the poor and optimal harnessing of scarce resources of water, air, energy, land, and bio-diversity will have to be sustained through more cooperative endeavours. Then alone we could make some headway in saving our lone planet from the brink of climate disasters.

1

CHAPTER

GLOBAL WARMING DEFINED

Global warming is the increase in the average temperature of Earth's near-surface air and oceans since the mid-20th century and its projected continuation. Global surface temperature increased 0.74 ± 0.18 °C (1.33 ± 0.32 °F) between the start and the end of the 20th century. The Intergovernmental Panel on Climate Change (IPCC) concludes that most of the observed temperature increase since the middle of the 20th century was very likely caused by increasing concentrations of greenhouse gases resulting from human activity such as fossil fuel burning and deforestation. The IPCC also concludes that variations in natural phenomena such as solar radiation and volcanic eruptions had a small cooling effect after 1950. These basic conclusions have been endorsed by more than 40 scientific societies and academies of science, including all of the national academies of science of the major industrialized countries.

Climate model projections summarized in the latest IPCC report indicate that the global surface temperature is likely to rise a further 1.1 to 6.4 °C (2.0 to 11.5 °F) during the 21st century. The uncertainty in this estimate arises from the use of models with differing sensitivity to greenhouse gas concentrations and the use of differing estimates of future greenhouse gas emissions. Most studies focus on the period leading up to the year 2100. However, warming is expected to continue beyond 2100 even if emissions stop, because of the large heat capacity of the oceans and the long lifetime of carbon dioxide in the atmosphere.

An increase in global temperature will cause sea levels to rise and will change the amount and pattern of precipitation, probably including expansion of subtropical deserts. Warming is expected to be strongest in the Arctic and would be associated with continuing retreat of glaciers, permafrost and sea ice. Other likely effects include changes in the frequency and intensity of extreme weather events, species extinctions, and changes in agricultural yields. Warming and related changes will vary from region to region around the globe, though the nature of these regional variations is uncertain.

Political and public debate continues regarding global warming, its causes and what actions to take in response. The available options are mitigation to reduce further emissions; adaptation to reduce the damage caused by warming; and, more speculatively, geoengineering to reverse global warming. Most national governments have signed and ratified the Kyoto Protocol aimed at reducing greenhouse gas emissions.

Temperature Changes

Evidence for warming of the climate system includes observed increases in global average air and ocean temperatures, widespread melting of snow and ice, and rising global average sea level. The most common measure of global warming is the trend in globally averaged temperature near the Earth's surface. Expressed as a linear trend, this temperature rose by 0.74 ± 0.18 °C over the period 1906–2005. The rate of warming over the last half of that period was almost double that for the period as a whole (0.13 ± 0.03 °C per decade, versus 0.07 °C ± 0.02 °C per decade). The urban heat island effect is estimated to account for about 0.002 °C of warming per decade since 1900. Temperatures in the lower troposphere have increased between 0.13 and 0.22 °C (0.22 and 0.4 °F) per decade since 1979, according to satellite temperature measurements. Temperature is believed to have been relatively stable over the one or two thousand years before 1850, with regionally varying fluctuations such as the Medieval Warm Period and the Little Ice Age.

Estimates by NASA's Goddard Institute for Space Studies and the National Climatic Data Center show that 2005 was the warmest year since reliable, widespread instrumental measurements became available in the late 1800s, exceeding the previous record set in 1998 by a few hundredths of a degree. Estimates prepared by the World Meteorological Organization and the Climatic Research Unit show 2005 as the second warmest year, behind 1998. Temperatures in 1998 were unusually warm because the strongest El Niño in the past century occurred during that year. Global temperature is subject to short-term fluctuations that overlay long term trends and can temporarily mask them. The relative stability in temperature from 2002 to 2009 is consistent with such an episode.

Temperature changes vary over the globe. Since 1979, land temperatures have increased about twice as fast as ocean temperatures (0.25 °C per decade against 0.13 °C per decade). Ocean temperatures increase more slowly than land temperatures because of the larger effective heat capacity of the oceans and because the ocean loses more heat by evaporation. The Northern Hemisphere warms faster than the Southern Hemisphere because it has more land and because it has extensive areas of seasonal snow and sea-ice cover subject to ice-albedo feedback. Although more greenhouse gases are emitted in the Northern than Southern Hemisphere this does not contribute to the difference in warming because the major greenhouse gases persist long enough to mix between hemispheres.

The thermal inertia of the oceans and slow responses of other indirect effects mean that climate can take centuries or longer to adjust to changes in forcing. Climate commitment studies indicate that even if greenhouse gases were stabilized at 2000 levels, a further warming of about 0.5 °C (0.9 °F) would still occur.

External forcing refers to processes external to the climate system (though not necessarily external to Earth) that influence climate. Climate responds to several types of external forcing, such as radiative forcing due to changes in atmospheric composition (mainly greenhouse gas concentrations), changes in solar luminosity, volcanic eruptions, and variations in Earth's orbit around the Sun. Attribution of recent climate change focuses on the first three types of forcing. Orbital cycles vary slowly over tens of thousands of years and thus are too gradual to have caused the temperature changes observed in the past century.

Greenhouse Gases

The greenhouse effect is the process by which absorption and emission of infrared radiation by gases in the atmosphere warm a planet's lower atmosphere and surface. It was discovered by Joseph Fourier in 1824 and was first investigated quantitatively by Svante Arrhenius in 1896. Existence of the greenhouse effect as such is not disputed, even by those who do not agree that the recent temperature increase is attributable to human activity. The question is instead how the strength of the greenhouse effect changes when human activity increases the concentrations of greenhouse gases in the atmosphere.

Naturally occurring greenhouse gases have a mean warming effect of about 33 °C (59 °F). The major greenhouse gases are water vapor, which causes about 36–70 percent of the greenhouse effect; carbon dioxide (CO_2), which causes 9–26 percent; methane (CH_4), which causes 4–9 percent; and ozone (O_3), which causes 3–7 percent. Clouds also affect the radiation balance, but they are composed of liquid water or ice and so have different effects on radiation from water vapor.

Human activity since the Industrial Revolution has increased the amount of greenhouse gases in the atmosphere, leading to increased radiative forcing from CO_2, methane, tropospheric ozone, CFCs and nitrous oxide. The concentrations of CO_2 and methane have increased by 36 percent and 148 percent respectively since 1750. These levels are much higher than at any time during the last 650,000 years, the period for which reliable data has been extracted from ice cores. Less direct geological evidence indicates that CO_2 values higher than this were last seen about 20 million years ago. Fossil fuel burning has produced about three-quarters of the increase in CO_2 from human activity over the past 20 years. Most of the rest is due to land-use change, particularly deforestation.

CO_2 concentrations are continuing to rise due to burning of fossil fuels and land-use change. The future rate of rise will depend on uncertain economic, sociological, technological, and natural developments. Accordingly, the IPCC Special Report on Emissions Scenarios gives a wide range of future

CO_2 scenarios, ranging from 541 to 970 ppm by the year 2100 (an increase by 90-250% since 1750). Fossil fuel reserves are sufficient to reach these levels and continue emissions past 2100 if coal, tar sands or methane clathrates are extensively exploited.

The destruction of stratospheric ozone by chlorofluorocarbons is sometimes mentioned in relation to global warming. Although there are a few areas of linkage, the relationship between the two is not strong. Reduction of stratospheric ozone has a cooling influence, but substantial ozone depletion did not occur until the late 1970s. Ozone in the troposphere (the lowest part of the Earth's atmosphere) does contribute to surface warming.

Aerosols and Soot

Global dimming, a gradual reduction in the amount of global direct irradiance at the Earth's surface, has partially counteracted global warming from 1960 to the present. The main cause of this dimming is aerosols produced by volcanoes and pollutants. These aerosols exert a cooling effect by increasing the reflection of incoming sunlight. James E. Hansen and colleagues have proposed that the effects of the products of fossil fuel combustion—CO_2 and aerosols—have largely offset one another in recent decades, so that net warming has been driven mainly by non-CO_2 greenhouse gases.

In addition to their direct effect by scattering and absorbing solar radiation, aerosols have indirect effects on the radiation budget. Sulfate aerosols act as cloud condensation nuclei and thus lead to clouds that have more and smaller cloud droplets. These clouds reflect solar radiation more efficiently than clouds with fewer and larger droplets. This effect also causes droplets to be of more uniform size, which reduces growth of raindrops and makes the cloud more reflective to incoming sunlight.

Soot may cool or warm, depending on whether it is airborne or deposited. Atmospheric soot aerosols directly absorb solar radiation, which heats the atmosphere and cools the surface. In isolated areas with high soot production, such as rural India, as much as 50 percent of surface warming due to greenhouse gases may be masked by atmospheric brown clouds. When deposited, especially on glaciers or on ice in arctic regions, the lower surface albedo can also directly heat the surface. The influences of aerosols, including black carbon, are most pronounced in the tropics and sub-tropics, particularly in Asia, while the effects of greenhouse gases are dominant in the extra tropics and southern hemisphere.

Solar Variation

Variations in solar output have been the cause of past climate changes. The consensus among climate scientists is that changes in solar forcing probably had a slight cooling effect in recent decades. This result is less certain than some others, with a few papers suggesting a warming effect.

Greenhouse gases and solar forcing affect temperatures in different ways. While both increased solar activity and increased greenhouse gases are expected to warm the troposphere, an increase in solar activity should warm the stratosphere while an increase in greenhouse gases should cool the stratosphere. Observations show that temperatures in the stratosphere have been cooling since 1979, when satellite measurements became available. Radiosonde (weather balloon) data from the pre-satellite era show cooling since 1958, though there is greater uncertainty in the early radiosonde record.

A related hypothesis, proposed by Henrik Svensmark, is that magnetic activity of the sun deflects cosmic rays that may influence the generation of cloud condensation nuclei and thereby affect the climate. Other research has found no relation between warming in recent decades and cosmic rays. A recent study concluded that the influence of cosmic rays on cloud cover is about a factor of 100 lower than needed to explain the observed changes in clouds or to be a significant contributor to present-day climate change.

Feedback

Feedback is a process in which changing one quantity changes a second quantity, and the change in the second quantity in turn changes the first. Positive feedback amplifies the change in the first quantity while negative feedback reduces it. Feedback is important in the study of global warming because it may amplify or diminish the effect of a particular process. The main positive feedback in global warming is the tendency of warming to increase the amount of water vapor in the atmosphere, a significant greenhouse gas. The main negative feedback is radiative cooling, which increases as the fourth power of temperature; the amount of heat radiated from the Earth into space increases with the temperature of Earth's surface and atmosphere. Imperfect understanding of feedbacks is a major cause of uncertainty and concern about global warming.

Climate Models

The geographic distribution of surface warming during the 21st century calculated by the HadCM3 climate model if a business as usual scenario is assumed for economic growth and greenhouse gas emissions. In this figure, the globally averaged warming corresponds to 3.0 °C (5.4 °F).

The main tools for projecting future climate changes are mathematical models based on physical principles including fluid dynamics, thermodynamics and radiative transfer. Although they attempt to include as many processes as possible, simplifications of the actual climate system are inevitable because of the constraints of available computer power and limitations in knowledge of the climate system. All modern climate models are in fact combinations of models for different parts of the Earth. These include an atmospheric model for air movement, temperature, clouds, and other atmospheric properties; an ocean model that predicts temperature, salt content, and circulation of ocean waters; models for ice cover on land and sea; and a model of heat and moisture transfer from soil and vegetation to the atmosphere. Some models also include treatments of chemical and biological processes. Warming due to increasing levels of greenhouse gases is not an assumption of the models; rather, it is an end result from the interaction of greenhouse gases with radiative transfer and other physical processes. Although much of the variation in model outcomes depends on the greenhouse gas emissions used as inputs, the temperature effect of a specific greenhouse gas concentration (climate sensitivity) varies depending on the model used. The representation of clouds is one of the main sources of uncertainty in present-generation models.

Global climate model projections of future climate most often have used estimates of greenhouse gas emissions from the IPCC Special Report on Emissions Scenarios (SRES). In addition to human-caused emissions, some models also include a simulation of the carbon cycle; this generally shows a positive feedback, though this response is uncertain. Some observational studies also show a positive feedback. Including uncertainties in future greenhouse gas concentrations and climate sensitivity, the IPCC anticipates a warming of 1.1 °C to 6.4 °C (2.0 °F to 11.5 °F) by the end of the 21st century, relative to 1980–1999.

Models are also used to help investigate the causes of recent climate change by comparing the observed changes to those that the models project from various natural and human-derived causes. Although these models do not unambiguously attribute the warming that occurred from approximately 1910 to 1945 to either natural variation or human effects, they do indicate that the warming since 1970 is dominated by man-made greenhouse gas emissions.

The physical realism of models is tested by examining their ability to simulate current or past climates. Current climate models produce a good match to observations of global temperature changes over the last century, but do not simulate all aspects of climate. Not all effects of global warming are accurately predicted by the climate models used by the IPCC. For example, observed Arctic shrinkage has been faster than that predicted.

2

CHAPTER

CAUSES OF GLOBAL WARMING

Global warming is a major issue due to the industrialization and progress by humankind since the past few years. There has been a hue and cry about global warming ever since the idea was first put forward. There are many articles on global warming on the Internet as well as print media which give further details about the causes of global warming. Here is some further information on global warming. Global warming has been and is being caused due to various factors. Global warming is basically a change in the climatic conditions of the earth. These climatic conditions vary due to various reasons---external and internal. Changes to climatic conditions and, therefore, global warming can be caused due to natural or man-made circumstances also. Some of the factors causing global warming are volcanic emissions and solar activity. According to the solar variation theory, the sun has been gaining strength and is at its strongest. Therefore, it may now be acting as a cause of global warming. Sunspots are also said to be a cause or catalyst for global warming. Recent reports suggest that the number of sunspots in an area directly affects the amount of time the nearby earth takes to cool. The sun is the main source of energy to the earth. The earth absorbs about seventy percent of the earth's solar flux. This solar flux increases the temperature of the earth's atmosphere, land and oceans.

Orbital forcing is also said to be one of the natural causes of global warming. The reports show the effect of the slow tilting of the earth's axis on the climate of the earth. The greenhouse effect is said to be the most important factor regarding global warming. When infrared radiation from the atmosphere increases the temperature of the earth's surface, it is termed as the greenhouse effect. The greenhouse effect has increased the earth's temperature by about twenty-four percent. Carbon dioxide contributes about twelve percent of the greenhouse effect, while water vapour contributes thirty-six percent of the greenhouse effect. Methane causes five to ten percent of global warming, while ozone makes around three to seven percent of the greenhouse effect possible. Solar variation is said to be another reason of global warming. The changes in the amount of radiant energy emitted by the sun are known as solar variation. This solar variation has been correlated with the changes in the earth's climate and temperature. Along with the natural causes of global warming, scientists have also contributed rapid industrialization to the increase of global warming today. Humans had first affected global warming some eight thousand years ago, with the start of agriculture. Due to the clearing of the forests for agriculture, the amount of carbon dioxide in the atmosphere increased drastically. Scientists are of the opinion that industrialization releases various gases like carbon-dioxide and methane which are known to contribute to global warming. Deforestation is also said to increase global warming. Trees contain a high level of carbon, and therefore their cutting creates an increase of carbon in the atmosphere. Humankind also contributes to the increase of carbon dioxide by the burning of fossil fuels. The contribution of mankind to global warming due to the burning of fossil fuels has increased by about eighty percent in the past twenty years.

If the greenhouse effect didn't exist, the temperature of the earth would be around less than twenty seven Celsius. Some scientists are of the opinion that human life would be impossible on earth if the temperature would be so less. It is, first of all, the types of technology and energy that we use to power our industrialized lifestyles, and, second, the way we use our land, that are causing pollution and driving the process of global warming. Fundamental Causes of Global Warming It is not a surprise that global warming is the result of human-induced pollution. As we have seen before, there are many types of environmental pollution and specifically air pollution, which negatively affect the health of the environment but do not directly contribute to global warming. Instead, the main immediate global warming cause is the increased concentration of greenhouse gases in the atmosphere. The greenhouse gases are the by-products of many human activities.

Once emitted, some of these greenhouse gases end up in the atmosphere, where they trap a certain amount of originally solar energy (which would have otherwise escaped to space), and thus radiate this energy back to the earth raising the planet's average temperature. So, the first fundamental global warming cause is an absolute dependence of the modern human society on the burning of fossil fuels, which is the most important source of greenhouse gas emissions. The focal point of this cause is the generation of energy for use both in industry and commercial/private sector. Fossil fuel combustion is especially heavily used as a source of energy for industry.

In fact, industry literally cannot exist without fossil fuels. Carbon dioxide (CO_2) is the main greenhouse gas emitted as a by-product of fossil fuel combustion. This gas is the most important immediate global warming cause. Some amounts of carbon dioxide are removed from the atmosphere by the carbon sinks, such as tropical rainforests and oceans, as part of the process of carbon exchange between the atmosphere and the earth ("carbon cycle"). This carbon exchange has been taking place for thousands of years. It is an implicit guarantor of the earth's climate stability since the amount of carbon on the planet is more or less constant. Carbon is, indeed, "the chemical basis of all known life." The carbon content of past living organisms has been stored in the form of fossil fuels—oil, gas and coal—which we use in virtually every aspect of our lives. But the problem is that, as Barry Commoner notes: "The amounts of these fuels burned to provide society with energy represent the carbon captured by photosynthesis over millions of years. So, by burning them...we have returned carbon dioxide to the atmosphere thousands of times faster than the rate at which it was removed by the early tropical forests." In other words, we now release very large amounts of carbon dioxide at a very high rate, and the nature is unable to remove it in good time. This leads to the accumulation of extra carbon in the atmosphere and, consequently, to global warming. We have some other industry-related activities (usually called industrial processes) which are also significant sources of greenhouse gases such as fluorocarbons, carbon dioxide as well as small amounts of methane (CH) and nitrous oxide (N,0).

The products whose manufacturing causes the emission of these gases include cement, minerals, chemicals, metals, etc. Many activities related to industrial processes use large amounts of energy and thus produce significant amounts of greenhouse gas emissions through fossil fuel combustion. But industrial processes also produce greenhouse emissions not related to fossil fuel combustion but rather related to the use of specific methods and materials for the manufacture of the products mentioned above. So the first global warming cause is related to activities which are performed to generate the energy needed for industry and commercial and private sectors. The second fundamental global warming cause is related to the way we use our land, i.e. landuse. Among other applications, most common landuse activities include:

- Modern agricultural practices employed to breed animals, grow cereals, fruits and vegetables and other foods, all for human consumption. The two important greenhouse gases emitted by agricultural practices are methane (CH4) and nitrous oxide (N20). • Clearance of land for timber sales or for the expansion of human settlements /cattle ranches. Alongside a cocktail of pollution released as part of this process, the main greenhouse gas emitted is carbon dioxide (CO_2). A very important element of this area is tropical deforestation, especially by way of forest fires, which alongside other pollutants causes the release of carbon dioxide. A significant component related to but different from, landuse is waste management.

The main greenhouse gas emitted as a result of waste management activities is methane, with some small amounts of nitrous oxide. Natural Causes of Global Warming The following natural factors may cause an increase in the earth's temperature.

CHANGES IN SOLAR ENERGY OUTPUT

Since the sun is the only source of energy for the functioning of the earth's climate system, any changes in solar output may lead to climate change and, specifically global warming. It is predicted that a change in solar output by only one percent per century may change the average temperature of the planet by between 0.5 to 1.0°C.

CHANGES IN THE EARTH'S ORBITAL CHARACTERISTICS

Changes in the shape of the earth's orbit around the sun as well as the tilt of the earth's axis alter the total amount of solar energy received by the planet. This would also affect the planet's temperature.

SUMMARY OF IMPORTANT ANTHROPOGENIC GREENHOUSE GASES

So, among the most important anthropogenic greenhouse gases we have:

- Carbon dioxide (CO_2);
- Methane (CI-14);
- Nitrous oxide (N70);
- Fluorocarbons (including hydro fluorocarbons (1-IFCs) and
- Per fluorocarbons (PPCs)); and Sulphur hex a fluoride (S17,). Many of these gases come from natural sources.

But it is the human-caused contribution of these gases to global warming that we are interested in for the purposes of our discussion. We will focus on three greenhouse gases—carbon dioxide, methane and nitrous oxide—since they are the main anthropogenic contributors to global warming. Carbon dioxide is by far the most important past and current greenhouse gas, followed by methane and nitrous oxide.

According to the calculations of the potential impact of each greenhouse gas on the future global temperatures weighed by their global warming potential and based on the year 2000 emissions data, the contribution of each gas to the total temperature rise over the next 100 years is projected to be:

- Carbon dioxide-72 percent;
- Methane-19 percent; and
- Nitrous oxide-9 percent.

Although some non-greenhouse air pollutants do not directly contribute to global warming, once in the air they may be transformed into actual greenhouse gases (for example, carbon monoxide (CO) may be transformed into carbon dioxide (CO_2)) and thus indirectly contribute to global warming. Such non-greenhouse gases are called precursor gases. Some of the most important precursor gases are carbon monoxide (CO), nitrogen oxides (NOx) and volatile organic compounds (VOC). Major Economic Sectors Acting as Causes of Global Warming As we described above, energy and land activities are the major anthropogenic sources of greenhouse gas emissions, complemented by industrial processes and waste management.

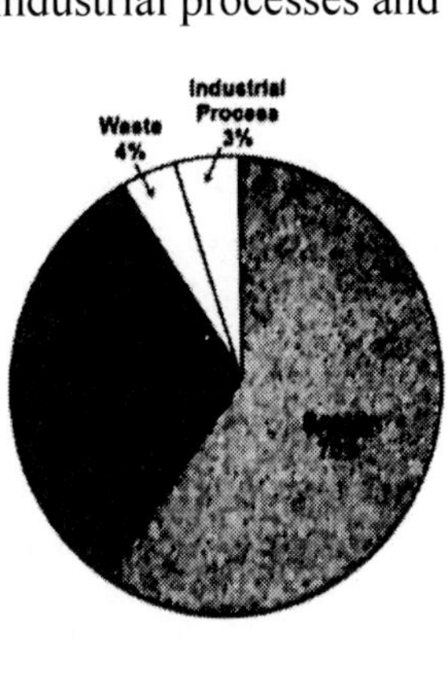

The pie chart shows the shares of each sector in the total amount of global greenhouse gas emissions (weighed by their global warming potential).

TABLE: 2.1

Total Greenhouse gas Emission by Different Sectors, as to 2000, Tg

Energy	28,642
Landuse	9,628
Waste	1,539
Ind. Processes	1,049
Total	40, 858

The energy sector is by far the largest emitter of greenhouse gases (70%) followed by the landuse sector (23%), waste management (4%) and industrial processes (3%). Below we analyse exactly which sub-sectors within each sector are the biggest emitters of certain greenhouse gases. As we can see, power generation is the biggest source of greenhouse gases (specifically, CO_2) within the energy sector, with 31 percent of the energy sector's total emissions. Power generation includes public electricity and heat production, according to the UNFCCC emissions reporting guidelines. A very significant proportion of power plants around the world depends on fossil fuels (coal, natural gas, oil) as their sources of energy.

And as we know, fossil fuel combustion is the primary global source of carbon dioxide, the most powerful of all greenhouse gases acting as causes of global warming. Coal is a particularly dirty fuel. It is not only a source of greenhouse gases, including carbon dioxide and methane, but also a source of other waste products such as heavy metals (including arsenic, lead, mercury, etc.) polluting the environment and resulting in radioactive waste.

TABLE: 2.2

Global Warming Cause: Energy Sector

Sub-Sector	**CO2**	**CH4**	**N2O (CO2eq)**	**Total**	**Total**
Power generation	8,814	3	30	8,847	31%
Industrial sector (excl. refineries etc)	4,398	8	9	4,415	15%
Road	4,276	22	32	4,329	15%
Residential, commercial and other sectors	3,390	42	7	3,439	12%
Other transformation sector (incl. refineries etc)	2,222	9	5	2,236	8%
Gas production and transportation	0	1,235	0	1,235	4%
Non-energy use and chem. feedstocks (CO2 ONLY)	916	0	0	916	3%
Coal production	0	849	0	849	3%
Air	654	0	6	660	2%
Oil extraction, transportation and handling	291	262	0	554	2%
Intl. shipping	428	0	1	429	1%
Rail and other non-road	390	0	1	390	1%
Bio-fuel residential	0	345	0	345	1%
Total	25,778	2,774	90	28,642	100%

Many countries heavily depend on coal for power generation. For example, in 2006 coal was used to produce roughly 49 percent of total electricity capacity of the US. Developing countries such as Russia are especially dependent on coal as this resource is still in plenty. In addition to coal, natural gas and oil-based power plants are also serious sources of greenhouse gases. Industrial sector generates around 15 percent of the energy sector's total emissions and includes fossil fuel combustion to power primarily manufacturing industries such as iron and steel, chemical, paper production and other industries. Road transport is, of course, another major generator of greenhouse gas emissions (15% of the total amount), as still a vast majority of vehicles around the world are currently powered by liquid oil. Together these three sub-sectors—power generation, industrial sector and road transport—produce slightly more than 60 percent of the total greenhouse gas emissions related to the energy sector. Therefore, they act as major global warming causes. The biggest greenhouse gas emitted by the energy sector in general is, without doubt, carbon dioxide—it makes up 90 percent of all the greenhouse gas emissions. As for the landuse sector, deforestation, animal enteric fermentation and rice cultivation are the top three sub-sectors with the largest- greenhouse gas emissions. Deforestation. Causes 31 percent: of the total landuse emissions and is a very serious problem not only from the point of view of global warming but also in respect of irreversible plant and animal diversity loss with negative consequences for many different groups of people and the not as a whole.

Of carbon Since forests are one of the largest storages deforestation, particularly through forest fires, is a major; source of carbon dioxide emissions, globally. This is especially true for many tropical countries which are host to tropical rainforests and all the natural resources coming with them.

TABLE: 2.3

Global Warming Cause: Landuse Sector

Sub-Sector	**CO2**	**CH4 (CO2 eq)**	**N2O (CO2eq)**	**Total**	**%**
Deforestation, incl. tropical forest fires	2,740	243	28	3,011	31%
Animals, enteric fermentation	0	2,001	0	2,001	21%
Rice cultivation	0	984	0	984	10%
Arable land, Fertil-izer use	0	0	822	822	9%
Animals waste deposited to soil	0	0	796	796	8%
Leaching & run- off	0	0	573	573	6%
Crop production	0	0	467	467	5%
Animals waste Man-agement	0	212	166	378	4%
Savannah and shrubs fires	0	233	41	274	3%
Deforestation, post burning effects	0	0	181	181	2%
Atmospheric deposi-tion	0	0	115	115	1%
Total	2,740	3,6713	3,189	9,602	100%

Enteric fermentation by farm animals (such as cattle, sheep, goats etc.) is another important source of greenhouse emissions (21 percent of total landuse emissions). Enteric fermentation is a process through which animals produce methane in their digestive tract and then either belch it or pass it out as gas.

It is one of the reasons why there are now global calls to start abandoning meat-based diets in favour of vegetarian ones. Rice cultivation is one more major cause of methane ernic.

cions, producing 10 percent of total landuse emissions. There are several sub-sectors within the landuse sector which emit significant amounts of nitrous oxide. This is specifically true because of a widespread use of artificial fertilizers in agricultural production. The main greenhouse gases emitted by landuse activities are methane and nitrous oxide, with a significant amount of carbon dioxide produced as a result of deforestation.

TABLE : 2.4

Global Warming Causes: Industrial Processes

Sub-sector	CO2	CH4 (CO2eq)	N2O (CO2 eq)	Total	Total (%)
Building materials	826	0	0	826	79%
Chemicals	0	0	196	196	19%
Iron & Steel	0	21	0	21	2%
Solvent use	0	0	7	7	1%
Total	826	21	203	1,050	100%

For industrial processes, the most important sub-sector is building materials. It includes production of cement which generates a big share of the total global anthropogenic carbon dioxide emissions.

TABLE: 2.5

Global Warming Cause: waste Management Sector

Sub-Sector	CO2	CH4 (CO2eq)	N2O (CO2 eq)	Total	Total (%)
Human wastewater disposal	0	736	0	736	48%
Landfills	0	577	0	577	38%
Waster water treat-ment	0	135	85	220	14%
Total	0	1,448	85	1,532	100%

The main gas emitted by the waste management sector is methane. Deforestation as One of the Major Causes of Global Warming There is no doubt that over the last several decades deforestation has become one of the greatest sources of greenhouse gas emissions and, therefore, one of the most important contributors to global warming. Deforestation accounts for at least seven percent of the total global greenhouse gas emissions (though many sources often refer to a figure of 20 percent here-that depends on particular methodology applied to derive this figure), with the main gas being carbon dioxide plus smaller amounts of methane and nitrous oxide.

Tropical rainforests play a very important role in regulating global and regional climate patterns. So their destruction inevitably causes disruptions in many environmental services as well.

An extremely important service provided by the rainforests is the removal of carbon dioxide from the atmosphere by photosynthesis. In other words, it acts as a pollution /carbon dioxide sink and storage. So in global warming terms, deforestation leads to:

- Release of carbon dioxide from the trees back into the atmosphere;
- Release of carbon stores held in the soil into the atmosphere; Destruction of forests as carbon sinks for future carbon dioxide removal (i.e. damage to the planet's future "carbon-sequestration" potential); and
- All the above will further contribute to the global Warming effect.

However, the global warming effect from deforestation may be counterbalanced by the earth's increased albedo ratio. The higher albedo ratio means that the earth will be able to reflect more solar energy back into space and thus contribute to global cooling. The issue of deforestation has recently received a special international attention for several different reasons:

1. Deforestation is a source of greenhouse gas emissions and, therefore, global warming.
2. Environmental services provided by the rainforests benefit all the inhabitants of the planet rather than just citizens of the rainforest host countries.
3. It is very difficult to control deforestation on a local level.
4. The vast majority of earth's remaining forest cover is located in developing countries in the regions around the equator. These countries desperately need resources provided by the rainforests for their own economic and social developments. The challenge to the international community is to find sustainable ways of rainforest management which would guarantee economic development for host countries as well as rain forests' healthy functioning.

3

CHAPTER

EFFECTS OF GLOBAL WARMING

The effects, or impacts, of climate change may be physical, ecological, social or economic. Evidence of observed climate change includes the instrumental temperature record, rising sea levels, and decreased snow cover in the Northern Hemisphere. According to IPCC (2007a:10), "[most] of the observed increase in global average temperatures since the mid-20th century is *very likely* due to the observed increase in [human greenhouse gas] concentrations". It is predicted that future climate changes will include further global warming (i.e., an upward trend in global mean temperature), sea level rise, and a probable increase in the frequency of some extreme weather events. Signatories of the United Nations Framework Convention on Climate Change have agreed to implement policies designed to reduce their emissions of greenhouse gases.

Overview

Over the last hundred years or so, the instrumental temperature record has shown a trend in climate of increased global mean temperature, i.e., global warming. Other observed changes include Arctic shrinkage, Arctic methane release, releases of terrestrial carbon from permafrost regions and Arctic methane release in coastal sediments, and sea level rise. Global average temperature is predicted to increase over this century, with a probable increase in frequency of some extreme weather events, and changes in rainfall patterns. Moving from global to regional scales, there is increased uncertainty over how climate will change. The probability of warming having unforeseen consequences increases with the rate, magnitude, and duration of climate change.[6] Some of the physical impacts of climate change are irreversible at continental and global scales. With medium confidence, IPCC (2007b:17) concluded that with a global average temperature increase of 1–4°C, (relative to 1990–2000) partial deglaciation of the Greenland ice sheet would occur over a period of centuries to millennia. Including the possible contribution of partial deglaciation of the West Antarctic Ice Sheet, sea level would rise by 4–6 m or more.

The impacts of climate change across world population will not be distributed evenly (Smith *et al.*, 2001:957). Some regions and sectors are expected to experience benefits while others will experience costs. With greater levels of warming (greater than 2–3°C by 2100, relative to 1990 temperature levels), it is very likely that benefits will decline and costs increase (IPCC, 2007b:17). Low-latitude and less-developed areas are probably at the greatest risk from climate change (Schneider *et al.*, 2007:781). With human systems, adaptation potential for climate change impacts is considerable, although the costs of adaptation are largely unknown and potentially large. In a literature assessment, Schneider *et al.* (2007:792) concluded, with high confidence, that climate change would likely result in reduced diversity of ecosystems and the extinction of many species.

Climate change refers to a change in the state of the climate that can be identified by changes in the mean and/ or variability of its properties, and that persists for extended periods, typically decades or longer (IPCC, 2007d:30). The climate change referred to may be due to natural causes or the result of human activity.

Physical Impacts

This section describes physical impacts of climate change. For some of these physical impacts, their effect on social and economic systems are also described.

EFFECTS ON WEATHER

Increasing temperature is likely to lead to increasing precipitation but the effects on storms are less clear. Extratropical storms partly depend on the temperature gradient, which is predicted to weaken in the northern hemisphere as the polar region warms more than the rest of the hemisphere.

Extreme Weather

IPCC (2007a:8) predicted that in the future, over most land areas, the frequency of warm spells or heat waves would very likely increase. Other likely changes are listed below:

- Increased areas will be affected by drought;
- There will be increased intense tropical cyclone activity; and
- There will be increased incidences of extreme high sea level (excluding tsunamis).

Local Climate Change

Regional effects of global warming vary in nature. Some are the result of a generalised global change, such as rising temperature, resulting in local effects, such as melting ice. In other cases, a change may be related to a change in a particular ocean current or weather system. In such cases, the regional effect may be disproportionate and will not necessarily follow the global trend.

There are three major ways in which global warming will make changes to regional climate: melting or forming ice, changing the hydrological cycle (of evaporation and precipitation) and changing currents in the oceans and air flows in the atmosphere. The coast can also be considered a region, and will suffer severe impacts from sea level rise.

Biogeochemical Cycles

Climate change may have an effect on the carbon cycle in an interactive "feedback" process. A feedback exists where an initial process triggers changes in a second process that in turn influences the initial process. A positive feedback intensifies the original process, and a negative feedback reduces it (IPCC, 2007d:78). Models suggest that the interaction of the climate system and the carbon cycle is one where the feedback effect is positive (Schneider *et al.*, 2007:792).

Using the A2 SRES emissions scenario, Schneider *et al.* (2007:789) found that this effect led to additional warming by 2100, relative to the 1990-2000 period, of 0.1 to 1.5 °C. This estimate was made with high confidence. The climate projections made in the IPCC Forth Assessment Report of 1.1 to 6.4 °C account for this feedback effect. On the other hand, with medium confidence, Schneider *et al.* (2007) commented that additional releases of GHGs were possible from permafrost, peat lands, wetlands, and large stores of marine hydrates at high latitudes.

Glacier retreat and Disappearance

IPCC (2007a:5) found that, on average, mountain glaciers and snow cover had decreased in both the northern and southern hemispheres. This widespread decrease in glaciers and ice caps has contributed to observed sea level rise. With very high or high confidence, IPCC (2007d:11) made a number of predictions relating to future changes in glaciers:

- Mountainous areas in Europe will face glacier retreat
- In Latin America, changes in precipitation patterns and the disappearance of glaciers will significantly affect water availability for human consumption, agriculture, and energy production
- In Polar regions, there will be reductions in glacier extent and the thickness of glaciers.

Oceans

The role of the oceans in global warming is a complex one. The oceans serve as a sink for carbon dioxide, taking up much that would otherwise remain in the atmosphere, but increased levels of CO_2 have led to ocean acidification. Furthermore, as the temperature of the oceans increases, they become less able to absorb excess CO_2. Global warming is projected to have a number of effects on the oceans. Ongoing effects include rising sea levels due to thermal expansion and melting of glaciers and ice sheets, and warming of the ocean surface, leading to increased temperature stratification. Other possible effects include large-scale changes in ocean circulation.

Acidification

Dissolving CO_2 in seawater increases the hydrogen ion (H^+) concentration in the ocean, and thus decreases ocean pH.

Caldeira and Wickett (2003) placed the rate and magnitude of modern ocean acidification changes in the context of probable historical changes during the last 300 million years.[15] Since the industrial revolution began, it is estimated that surface ocean pH has dropped by slightly less than 0.1 units (on the logarithmic scale of pH; approximately a 25 percent increase in H^+), and it is estimated that it will drop by a further 0.3 to 0.5 units by 2100 as the oceans absorb more anthropogenic CO_2.

Oxygen Depletion

The amount of oxygen dissolved in the oceans may decline, with adverse consequences for ocean life.

Sea Level Rise

Sea level has been rising 0.2 cm/year, based on measurements of sea level rise from 23 long tide gauge records in geologically stable environments.

IPCC (2007a:5) reported that since 1961, global average sea level had risen at an average rate of 1.8 [1.3 to 2.3] mm/yr. Between 1993 and 2003, the rate increased above the previous period to 3.1 [2.4 to 3.8] mm/yr. IPCC (2007a) were uncertain whether the increase in rate from 1993 to 2003 was due to natural variations in sea level over the time period, or whether it reflected an increase in the underlying long-term trend.

IPCC (2007a:13, 14) projected sea level rise to the end of the 21st century using the SRES emission scenarios. Across the six SRES marker scenarios, sea level was projected to rise by 18 to 59 cm (7.1 to 23.2 inches). This projection was for the time period 2090-2099, with the increase in level relative to average sea levels over the 1980-1999 period. Due to a lack of scientific understanding, this sea level rise estimate does not include all of the possible contributions of ice sheets.

Shutdown of the Rmohaline Circulation

There is some speculation that global warming could, via a shutdown or slowdown of the thermohaline circulation, trigger localized cooling in the North Atlantic and lead to cooling, or lesser warming, in that region. This would affect in particular areas like Scandinavia and Britain that are warmed by the North Atlantic drift.

IPCC (2007b:17) concluded that a slowing of the Meridional Overturning Circulation would very likely occur this century. Due to global warming, temperatures across the Atlantic and Europe were still projected to increase.

Temperature Rise

From 1961 to 2003, the global ocean temperature has risen by 0.10 °C from the surface to a depth of 700 m. There is variability both year-to-year and over longer time scales, with global ocean heat content observations showing high rates of warming for 1991 to 2003, but some cooling from 2003 to 2007. The temperature of the Antarctic Southern Ocean rose by 0.17 °C (0.31 °F) between the 1950s and the 1980s, nearly twice the rate for the world's oceans as a whole. As well as having effects on ecosystems (e.g. by melting sea ice, affecting algae that grow on its underside), warming reduces the ocean's ability to absorb CO_2.

SOCIAL SYSTEMS

Food Supply

Climate change will impact agriculture and food production around the world due to: the effects of elevated CO_2 in the atmosphere, higher temperatures, altered precipitation and transpiration regimes, increased frequency of extreme events, and modified weed, pest, and pathogen pressure (Easterling *et al*., 2007:282). In general, low-latitude areas are at most risk of having decreased crop yields (Schneider *et al*., 2007:790). With low to medium confidence, Schneider *et al*. (2007:787) concluded that for about a 1 to 3°C global mean temperature increase (by 2100, relative to the 1990-2000 average level) there would be productivity decreases for some cereals in low latitudes, and productivity increases in high latitudes. With medium confidence, global production potential was predicted to:

- Increase up to around 3°C,
- Very likely decrease above about 3 to 4°C.

Most of the studies on global agriculture assessed by Schneider *et al*. (2007:790) had not incorporated a number of critical factors, including changes in extreme events, or the spread of pests and diseases. Studies had also not considered the development of specific practices or technologies to aid adaptation.

Health

Human beings are exposed to climate change through changing weather patterns (temperature, precipitation, sea-level rise and more frequent extreme events) and indirectly through changes in water, air and food quality and changes in ecosystems, agriculture, industry and settlements and the economy (Confalonieri *et al*., 2007:393). According to a literature assessment by Confalonieri *et al*. (2007:393), the effects of climate change to date have been small, but are projected to progressively increase in all countries and regions.

With high confidence, Confalonieri *et al*. (2007:393) concluded that climate change had altered the seasonal distribution of some allergenic pollen species. With medium confidence, they concluded that climate change had:

- Altered the distribution of some infectious disease vectors
- Increased heatwave-related deaths

With high confidence, IPCC (2007d:48) projected that:

- The health status of millions of people would be affected through, for example, increases in malnutrition; increased deaths, diseases and injury due to extreme weather events; increased burden of diarrhoeal diseases; increased frequency of cardio-respiratory diseases due to high concentrations of ground-level ozone in urban areas related to climate change; and altered spatial distribution of some infectious diseases.
- Climate change would bring some benefits in temperate areas, such as fewer deaths from cold exposure, and some mixed effects such as changes in range and transmission potential of malaria in Africa. Overall, IPCC (2007d:48) expected that benefits would be outweighed by negative health effects of rising temperatures, especially in developing countries.

With very high confidence, Confalonieri *et al.* (2007:393) concluded that economic development was an important component of possible adaptation to climate change. Economic growth on its own, however, was not judged to be sufficient to insulate the world's population from disease and injury due to climate change. The manner in which economic growth occurs was judged to be important, along with how the benefits of growth are distributed in society. Examples of other important factors in determining the health of populations were listed as: education, health care, and public-health infrastructure.

Water resources

In a literature assessment, Kundzewicz *et al.* (2007:175) concluded, with high confidence, that:

- The negative impacts of climate change on freshwater systems outweigh the benefits. All of the regions assessed in the IPCC Fourth Assessment Report (Africa, Asia, Australia and New Zealand, Europe, Latin America, North America, Polar regions (Arctic and Antarctic), and small islands) showed an overall net negative impact of climate change on water resources and freshwater ecosystems.

- Semi-arid and arid areas are particularly exposed to the impacts of climate change on freshwater. With very high confidence, it was judged that many of these areas, e.g., the Mediterranean basin, western USA, southern Africa, and north-eastern Brazil, would suffer a decrease in water resources due to climate change.

Migration and Conflict

An argument can be made that rising ethnic conflicts may be linked to competition over natural resources that are increasingly scarce as a result of climate change (Wilbanks *et al.*, 2007:365). According to a literature assessment by Wilbanks *et al.* (2007:365), other factors need to be taken into account. It was suggested that major environmentally-influenced conflicts in Africa have more to do with the relative abundance of resources, e.g., oil and diamonds, than with resource scarcity. On this basis, Wilbanks *et al.* (2007:365) suggested that predictions of future conflicts due climate change should be viewed with caution.

With high confidence, Schneider *et al.* (2007:787) predicted that stresses such as increased drought, water shortages, and riverine and coastal flooding would affect many local and regional populations. With medium confidence, it was predicted that these stresses would lead, in some cases, to relocation within or between countries. This might have the effect of exacerbating conflicts, and possibly impose migration pressures.

Aggregate Impacts

Aggregating impacts adds up the total impact of climate change across sectors and/or regions (IPCC, 2007d:76). The impacts of climate change across world population will not be distributed evenly (Smith *et al.*, 2001:957).[9] IPCC (2007b:17) found that for increases in global mean temperature of less than 1-3 °C above 1990 levels, some impacts were projected to produce benefits in some places and sectors, and produce costs in other places and sectors. For some low-latitude and polar regions, net costs were projected for small increases in temperature. According to IPCC (2007b:17), a temperature increase of greater than about 2-3 °C would very likely result in all regions either experiencing reductions in net benefits or increases in net costs.

Regions

Some regions are likely to be especially affected by climate change (IPCC, 2007d:9):

- The Arctic, because of high rates of projected warming.
- Africa, especially in the sub-Saharan region. This is due to the continent's low capacity to adapt to climate change and projected impacts.
- Small islands, due to high exposure of population and infrastructure at risk to sea-level rise and increased storm surge.
- Asian megadeltas, due to large populations and high exposure to sea-level rise, storm surge and river flooding.

Within other areas, some people are particularly at risk, such as the poor, young children and the elderly.

Biological Systems

With very high confidence, Schneider *et al.* (2007:792) concluded that regional temperature trends were already affecting species and ecosystems around the world. In a literature assessment, Rosenzweig *et al.* (2007:81) concluded that over the last three decades, human-induced warming had likely had a discernable influence on many physical and biological systems.

Schneider *et al.* (2007:792) concluded, with high confidence, that climate change would result in the extinction of many species and a reduction in the diversity of ecosystems.

- **Terrestrial ecosystems and biodiversity**: With a warming of 3°C, relative to 1990 levels, it is likely that global terrestrial vegetation would become a net source of carbon (Schneider *et al.*, 2007:792). With high confidence, Schneider *et al.* (2007:788) concluded that a global mean temperature increase of around 4°C (above the 1990-2000 level) by 2100 would lead to major extinctions around the globe.
- **Marine ecosystems and biodiversity**: With very high confidence, Schneider *et al.* (2007:792) concluded that a warming of 2°C above 1990 levels would result in mass mortality of coral reefs globally.
- **Freshwater ecosystems**: Above about a 4°C increase in global mean temperature by 2100 (relative to 1990-2000), Schneider *et al.* (2007:789) concluded, with high confidence, that many freshwater species would become extinct.

Environmental

Sparse records indicate that glaciers have been retreating since the early 1800s. In the 1950s measurements began that allow the monitoring of glacial mass balance, reported to the WGMS and the NSIDC.

It is usually impossible to connect specific weather events to global warming. Instead, global warming is expected to cause changes in the overall distribution and intensity of events, such as changes to the frequency and intensity of heavy precipitation. Broader effects are expected to include glacial retreat, Arctic shrinkage including long-term shrinkage of the Greenland ice sheet, and worldwide sea level rise. Some effects on both the natural environment and human life are, at least in part, already being attributed to global warming. A 2001 report by the IPCC suggests that glacier retreat, ice shelf disruption such as that of the Larsen Ice Shelf, sea level rise, changes in rainfall patterns, and increased intensity and frequency of extreme weather events are attributable in part to global warming. Other expected effects include water scarcity in some regions and increased precipitation in others, and changes in mountain snowpack.

Social and economic effects of global warming may be exacerbated by growing population densities in affected areas. It is expected that the health benefits of climate change (e.g., fewer deaths from cold exposure) will be outweighed by negative health effects (e.g., increased levels of malnutrition), especially in developing countries. A summary of probable effects and recent understanding can be found in the IPCC Fourth Assessment Report. According to this report, there is observational evidence for an increase in intense tropical cyclone activity in the North Atlantic Ocean since about 1970, in correlation with the increase in sea surface temperature (see Atlantic Multidecadal Oscillation), but that the detection of long-term trends is complicated by the quality of records prior to routine satellite observations. The summary also states that there is no clear trend in the annual worldwide number of tropical cyclones.

Additional expected effects include sea level rise of 0.18 to 0.59 meters (0.59 to 1.9 ft) in 2090–2100 relative to 1980–1999,[2] new trade routes resulting from arctic shrinkage, possible thermohaline circulation slowing, increasingly intense, in some locations, (but less frequent) hurricanes and extreme weather events, reductions in the ozone layer, changes in agriculture yields, and ocean oxygen depletion. Increased atmospheric CO_2 increases the amount of CO_2 dissolved in the oceans. CO_2 dissolved in the ocean reacts with water to form carbonic acid, resulting in ocean acidification. Ocean surface pH is estimated to have decreased from 8.25 near the beginning of the industrial era to 8.14 by 2004, and is projected to decrease by a further 0.14 to 0.5 units by 2100 as the ocean absorbs more CO_2. Heat and carbon dioxide trapped in the oceans may still take hundreds of years to be re-emitted, even after greenhouse gas emissions are eventually reduced. Since organisms and ecosystems are adapted to a narrow range of pH, this raises extinction concerns and disruptions in food webs. One study predicts 18 percent to 35 percent of a sample of 1,103 animal and plant species would be extinct by 2050, based on future climate projections. However, few mechanistic studies have documented extinctions due to recent climate change, and one study suggests that projected rates of extinction are uncertain.

Economic Impact

In a literature assessment, Smith and others concluded, with medium confidence, that:

- Climate change would increase income inequalities between and within countries;
- A small increase in global mean temperature (up to 2 °C by 2100, measured against 1990 levels) would result in net negative market sector impacts in many

developing countries and net positive market sector impacts in many developed countries; and

- The aggregate market sector impact (i.e., total impacts across all regions) of a small increase in global mean temperature would amount to plus or minus a few percent of world GDP.

With high confidence, Smith and others concluded that a medium (2-3 °C) to high (above 3 °C) level of warming would result in more intense negative impacts, and that net positive impacts would begin to decline and eventually become negative. They found that most studies showed aggregate net damages at a global scale above a medium temperature increase, with further damages at higher temperatures.

Depending on underlying assumptions, studies of the economic impacts of a doubling in atmospheric carbon dioxide (CO_2) from pre-industrial levels conclude that this would have a slightly negative to moderately positive aggregate effect on the agricultural sector. This aggregate effect hides substantial regional differences, with benefits mostly predicted in the developed world and strongly negative impacts for populations poorly connected to regional and global trading systems.

A number of other sectors will be affected by climate change, including the livestock, forestry, and fisheries industries. Other sectors sensitive to climate change include the energy, construction, insurance, tourism and recreation industries. The aggregate impact of climate change on most of these sectors is highly uncertain.

Stern in 2007 assessed climate change impacts using the basic economics of risk premiums. He found that unmitigated climate change could result in a reduction in welfare equivalent to a persistent average fall in global per-capita consumption of at least 5 percent. The study by Stern has received both criticism and support from other economists (see Stern Review). The IPCC in 2007 concluded that "Aggregate estimates of costs mask significant differences in impacts across sectors, regions and populations and *very likely* underestimate damage costs because they cannot include many non-quantifiable impacts."

4

CHAPTER

CLIMATE CHANGE AND AGRICULTURE

Climate change and agriculture are interrelated processes, both of which take place on a global scale. Global warming is projected to have significant impacts on conditions affecting agriculture, including temperature, carbon dioxide, glacial run-off, precipitation and the interaction of these elements. These conditions determine the carrying capacity of the biosphere to produce enough food for the human population and domesticated animals. The overall effect of climate change on agriculture will depend on the balance of these effects. Assessment of the effects of global climate changes on agriculture might help to properly anticipate and adapt farming to maximize agricultural production.

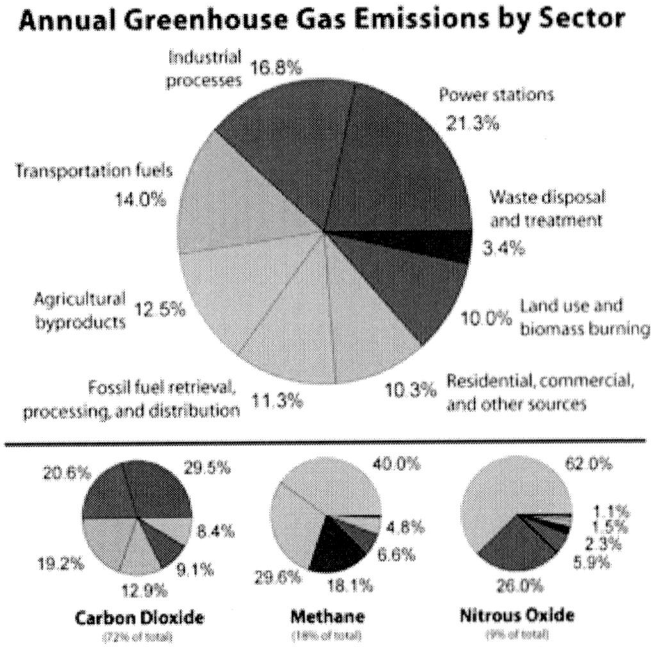

At the same time, agriculture has been shown to produce significant effects on climate change, primarily through the production and release of greenhouse gases such as carbon dioxide, methane, and nitrous oxide, but also by altering the Earth's land cover, which can change its ability to absorb or reflect heat and light, thus contributing to radiative forcing. Land use change such as deforestation and desertification, together with use of fossil fuels, are the major anthropogenic sources of carbon dioxide; agriculture itself is the major contributor to increasing methane and nitrous oxide concentrations in earth's atmosphere.

Impact of Climate Change on Agriculture

Despite technological advances, such as improved varieties, genetically modified organisms, and irrigation systems, weather is still a key factor in agricultural productivity, as well as soil properties and natural communities. The effect of climate on agriculture is related to variabilities in local climates rather than in global climate patterns. The Earth's average surface temperature has increased by 1 degree F in just over the last century. Consequently, agronomists consider any assessment has to be individually considering each local area.

On the other hand, agricultural trade has grown in recent years, and now provides significant amounts of food, on a national level to major importing countries, as well as comfortable income to exporting ones. The international aspect of trade and security in terms of food implies the need to also consider the effects of climate change on a global scale.

A study published in *Science* suggest that, due to climate change, "southern Africa could lose more than 30 percent of its main crop, maize, by 2030. In South Asia losses of many regional staples, such as rice, millet and maize could top 10 percent".

The 2001 IPCC Third Assessment Report concluded that the poorest countries would be hardest hit, with reductions in crop yields in most tropical and sub-tropical regions due to decreased water availability, and new or changed insect pest incidence. In Africa and Latin America many rain fed crops are near their maximum temperature tolerance, so that yields are likely to fall sharply for even small climate changes; falls in agricultural productivity of up to 30 percent over the 21st century are projected. Marine life and the fishing industry will also be severely affected in some places.

Climate change induced by increasing greenhouse gases is likely to affect crops differently from region to region. For example, average crop yield is expected to drop down to 50 percent in Pakistan according to the UKMO scenario whereas corn production in Europe is expected to grow up to 25 percent in optimum hydrologic conditions.

More favourable effects on yield tend to depend to a large extent on realization of the potentially beneficial effects of carbon dioxide on crop growth and increase of efficiency in water use. Decrease in potential yields is likely to be caused by shortening of the growing period, decrease in water availability and poor vernalization.

In the long run, the climatic change could affect agriculture in several ways :

- *Productivity*, in terms of quantity and quality of crops;
- *Agricultural practices*, through changes of water use (irrigation) and agricultural inputs such as herbicides, insecticides and fertilizers;
- *Environmental effects*, in particular in relation of frequency and intensity of soil drainage (leading to nitrogen leaching), soil erosion, reduction of crop diversity;
- *Rural space*, through the loss and gain of cultivated lands, land speculation, land renunciation, and hydraulic amenities; and
- *Adaptation*, organisms may become more or less competitive, as well as humans may develop urgency to develop more competitive organisms, such as flood resistant or salt resistant varieties of rice.

They are large uncertainties to uncover, particularly because there is lack of information on many specific local regions, and include the uncertainties on magnitude of climate change, the effects of technological changes on productivity, global food demands, and the numerous possibilities of adaptation.

Most agronomists believe that agricultural production will be mostly affected by the severity and pace of climate change, not so much by gradual trends in climate. If change is gradual, there may be enough time for biota adjustment. Rapid climate change, however, could harm agriculture in many countries, especially those that are already suffering from rather poor soil and climate conditions, because there is less time for optimum natural selection and adaption.

Projections

Schneider *et al.* (2007:787) assessed the literature on key vulnerabilities to climate change. With low to medium confidence, they concluded that for about a 1 to 3°C global mean temperature increase (by 2100, relative to the 1990-2000 average level) there would be productivity decreases for some cereals in low latitudes, and productivity increases in high latitudes. With medium confidence, global production potential was predicted to:

- increase up to around 3°C,
- very likely decrease above about 3 to 4°C.

Most of the studies on global agriculture assessed by Schneider *et al.* (2007:790) had not incorporated a number of critical factors, including changes in extreme events, or the spread of pests and diseases. Studies had also not considered the development of specific practices or technologies to aid adaptation.

REGIONAL

- **Africa:**
  - ♦ Africa's geography makes it particularly vulnerable to climate change, and seventy per cent of the population

rely on rain-fed agriculture for their livelihoods. Tanzania's official report on climate change suggests that the areas that usually get two rainfalls in the year will probably get more, and those that get only one rainy season will get far less. The net result is expected to be that 33 percent less maize—the country's staple crop—will be grown. Alongside other factors, regional climate change - in particular, reduced precipitation - is thought to have contributed to the conflict in Darfur. The combination of decades of drought, desertification and overpopulation are among the causes of the conflict, because the Baggara Arab nomads searching for water have to take their livestock further south, to land mainly occupied by farming peoples.

♦ With high confidence, IPCC (2007:13) concluded that climate variability and change would severely compromise agricultural production and access to food.

• **Asia**: With medium confidence, IPCC (2007:13) projected that by the mid-21st century, in East and Southeast Asia, crop yields could increase up to 20 percent, while in Central and South Asia, yields could decrease by up to 30 percent. Taken together, the risk of hunger was projected to remain very high in several developing countries.

• **Australia and New Zealand**: Hennessy *et al.*. (2007:509) assessed the literature for this region. They concluded that without further adaptation to climate change, projected impacts would likely be substantial: By 2030, production from agriculture and forestry was projected to decline over much of southern and eastern Australia, and over parts of eastern New Zealand; In New Zealand, initial benefits were projected close to major rivers and in western and southern areas. Hennessy *et al.* (2007:509) placed high confidence in these projections.

- **Europe**: With high confidence, IPCC (2007:14) projected that in Southern Europe, climate change would reduce crop productivity. In Central and Eastern Europe, forest productivity was expected to decline. In Northern Europe, the initial effect of climate change was projected to increase crop yields.
- **Latin America**: With high confidence, IPCC (2007:14) projected that in drier areas of Latin America, productivity of some important crops would decrease and livestock productivity decline, with adverse consequences for food security. In temperate zones, soybean yields were projected to increase.
- **North America**:
  - ♦ According to a paper by Deschenes and Greenstone (2006), predicted increases in temperature and precipitation will have virtually no effect on the most important crops in the US.
  - ♦ With high confidence, IPCC (2007:14-15) projected that over the first few decades of this century, moderate climate change would increase aggregate yields of rain-fed agriculture by 5–20 percent, but with important variability among regions. Major challenges were projected for crops that are near the warm end of their suitable range or which depend on highly utilized water resources.
- **Polar regions (Arctic and Antarctic)**:
  - ♦ For the *Guardian* newspaper, Brown (2005) reported on how climate change had affected agriculture in Iceland. Rising temperatures had made the widespread sowing of barley possible, which had been untenable twenty years ago. Some of the warming was due to a local (possibly temporary) effect via ocean currents from the Caribbean, which had also affected fish stocks.

- Anisimov *et al.*. (2007:655) assessed the literature for this region. With medium confidence, they concluded that the benefits of a less severe climate were dependent on local conditions. One of these benefits was judged to be increased agricultural and forestry opportunities.

- **Small islands**: In a literature assessment, Mimura *et al.* (2007:689) concluded, with high confidence, that subsistence and commercial agriculture would very likely be adversely affected by climate change.

Shortage in Grain Production

Crops such as these sunflowers can be affected by severe drought conditions in Australia.

Between 1996 and 2003, grain production has stabilized slightly over 1800 millions of tons. In 2000, 2001, 2002 and 2003, grain stocks have been dropping, resulting in a global grain harvest that was short of consumption by 93 millions of tons in 2003.

The Earth's average temperature has been rising since the late 1970s, with nine of the 10 warmest years on record occurring since 1995. In 2002, India and the United States suffered sharp harvest reductions because of record temperatures and drought. In 2003 Europe suffered very low rainfall throughout spring and summer, and a record level of heat damaged most crops from the United Kingdom and France in the Western Europe through Ukraine in the East. Bread prices have been rising in several countries in the region.

Poverty Impacts

Researchers at the Overseas Development Institute (ODI) have investigated the potential impacts climate change could have on agriculture, and how this would affect attempts at alleviating poverty in the developing world. They argued that the effects from moderate climate change are likely to be mixed for developing countries. However, the vulnerability of the poor in developing countries to short term impacts from climate change, notably the increased frequency and severity of adverse weather events is likely to have a negative impact. This, they say, should be taken into account when defining agricultural policy.

Crop Development Models

Models for climate behavior are frequently inconclusive. In order to further study effects of global warming on agriculture, other types of models, such as *crop development models*, *yield prediction*, quantities of *water or fertilizer consumed*, can be used. Such models condense the knowledge accumulated of the climate, soil, and effects observed of the results of various agricultural practices. They thus could make it possible to test strategies of adaptation to modifications of the environment.

Because these models are necessarily simplifying natural conditions (often based on the assumption that weeds, disease and insect pests are controlled), it is not clear whether the results they give will have an *in-field* reality. However, some results are partly validated with an increasing number of experimental results.

Other models, such as *insect and disease development* models based on climate projections are also used (for example simulation of aphid reproduction or septoria (cereal fungal disease) development).

Scenarios are used in order to estimate climate changes effects on crop development and yield. Each scenario is defined as a set of meteorological variables, based on generally accepted projections. For example, many models are running simulations based on doubled carbon dioxide projections, temperatures raise ranging from 1°C up to 5°C, and with rainfall levels an increase or decrease of 20 percent. Other parameters may include humidity, wind, and solar activity. Scenarios of crop models are testing farm-level adaptation, such as sowing date shift, climate adapted species (vernalisation need, heat and cold resistance), irrigation and fertilizer adaptation, resistance to disease. Most developed models are about wheat, maize, rice and soybean.

Temperature Potential Effect on Growing Period

Duration of crop growth cycles are above all, related to temperature. An increase in temperature will speed up development. In the case of an annual crop, the duration between sowing and harvesting will shorten (for example, the duration in order to harvest corn could shorten between one and four weeks). The shortening of such a cycle could have an adverse effect on productivity because senescence would occur sooner.

Effect of Elevated Carbon Dioxide on Crops

Carbon dioxide is essential to plant growth. Rising CO_2 concentration in the atmosphere can have both positive and negative consequences.

Increased CO_2 is expected to have positive physiological effects by increasing the rate of photosynthesis. Currently, the amount of carbon dioxide in the atmosphere is 380 parts per million. In comparison, the amount of oxygen is 210,000 ppm. This means that often plants may be starved of carbon dioxide, due to the enzyme that fixes CO_2, rubisco also fixes oxygen in the process of photorespiration. The effects of an increase in carbon dioxide would be higher on C3 crops (such as wheat) than on C4 crops (such as maize), because the former is more susceptible to carbon dioxide shortage. Studies have shown that increased CO_2 leads to fewer stomata developing on plants[19] which leads to reduced water usage. Under optimum conditions of temperature and humidity, the yield increase could reach 36 percent, if the levels of carbon dioxide are doubled.

Further, few studies have looked at the impact of elevated carbon dioxide concentrations on whole farming systems. Most models study the relationship between CO_2 and productivity in isolation from other factors associated with climate change, such as an increased frequency of extreme weather events, seasonal shifts, and so on.

In 2005, the Royal Society in London concluded that the purported benefits of elevated carbon dioxide concentrations are "likely to be far lower than previously estimated" when factors such as increasing ground-level ozone are taken into account."

Effect on Quality

According to the IPCC's TAR, "The importance of climate change impacts on grain and forage quality emerges from new research. For rice, the amylose content of the grain—a major determinant of cooking quality—is increased under elevated CO_2" (Conroy et al., 1994). Cooked rice grain from plants grown in high-CO_2 environments would be firmer than that from today's plants. However, concentrations of iron and zinc, which are important for human nutrition, would be lower (Seneweera and Conroy, 1997). Moreover, the protein content of the grain decreases under combined increases of temperature and CO_2 (Ziska et al., 1997)." Studies using FACE have shown that increases in CO_2 lead to decreased concentrations of micronutrients in crop plants.[23] This may have knock-on effects on other parts of ecosystems as herbivores will need to eat more food to gain the same amount of protein.

Studies have shown that higher CO_2 levels lead to reduced plant uptake of nitrogen (and a smaller number showing the same for trace elements such as zinc) resulting in crops with lower nutritional value. This would primarily impact on populations in poorer countries less able to compensate by eating more food, more varied diets, or possibly taking supplements.

Reduced nitrogen content in grazing plants has also been shown to reduce animal productivity in sheep, which depend on microbes in their gut to digest plants, which in turn depend on nitrogen intake.

Agricultural Surfaces and Climate Changes

Climate change may increase the amount of arable land in high-latitude region by reduction of the amount of frozen lands. A 2005 study reports that temperature in siberia has increased three degree Celsius in average since 1960 (much more than the rest of the world). However, reports about the impact of global warming on Russian agriculture indicate conflicting probable effects : while they expect a northward extension of farmable lands, they also warn of possible productivity losses and increased risk of drought.

Sea levels are expected to get up to one meter higher by 2100, though this projection is disputed. A rise in the sea level would result in an agricultural land loss, in particular in areas such as South East Asia. Erosion, submergence of shorelines, salinity of the water table due to the increased sea levels, could mainly affect agriculture through inundation of low-lying lands.

Low lying areas such as Bangladesh, India and Vietnam will experience major loss of rice crop if sea levels are expected to rise by the end of the century. Vietnam for example relies heavily on its southern tip, where the Mekong Delta lies, for rice planting. Any rise in sea level of no more than a meter will drown several km^2. of rice paddies, rendering Vietnam incapable of producing its main staple and export of rice.

Erosion and Fertility

The warmer atmospheric temperatures observed over the past decades are expected to lead to a more vigorous hydrological cycle, including more extreme rainfall events. Erosion and soil degradation is more likely to occur. Soil fertility would also be affected by global warming. However, because the ratio of carbon to nitrogen is a constant, a doubling of carbon is likely to imply a higher storage of nitrogen in soils as nitrates, thus providing higher fertilizing elements for plants, providing better yields. The average needs for nitrogen could decrease, and give the opportunity of changing often costly fertilisation strategies.

Due to the extremes of climate that would result, the increase in precipitations would probably result in greater risks of erosion, whilst at the same time providing soil with better hydration, according to the intensity of the rain. The possible evolution of the organic matter in the soil is a highly contested issue: while the increase in the temperature would induce a greater rate in the production of minerals, lessening the soil organic matter content, the atmospheric CO_2 concentration would tend to increase it.

Potential Effects of Global Climate Change on Pests, Diseases and Weeds

A very important point to consider is that weeds would undergo the same acceleration of cycle as cultivated crops, and would also benefit from carbonaceous fertilization. Since most weeds are C3 plants, they are likely to compete even more than now against C4 crops such as tomatoes. However, on the other hand, some results make it possible to think that weedkillers could gain in effectiveness with the temperature increase.

Global warming would cause an increase in rainfall in some areas, which would lead to an increase of atmospheric humidity and the duration of the wet seasons. Combined with higher temperatures, these could favor the development of fungal diseases. Similarly, because of higher temperatures and humidity, there could be an increased pressure from insects and disease vectors.

Glacier Retreat and Disappearance

The continued retreat of glaciers will have a number of different quantitative impacts. In areas that are heavily dependent on water runoff from glaciers that melt during the warmer summer months, a continuation of the current retreat will eventually deplete the glacial ice and substantially reduce or eliminate runoff. A reduction in runoff will affect the ability to irrigate crops and will reduce summer stream flows necessary to keep dams and reservoirs replenished.

Approximately 2.4 billion people live in the drainage basin of the Himalayan rivers. India, China, Pakistan, Afghanistan, Bangladesh, Nepal and Myanmar could experience floods followed by severe droughts in coming decades. In India alone, the Ganges provides water for drinking and farming for more than 500 million people. The west coast of North America, which gets much of its water from glaciers in mountain ranges such as the Rocky Mountains and Sierra Nevada, also would be affected.

Ozone and UV-B

Some scientists think agriculture could be affected by any decrease in stratospheric ozone, which could increase biologically dangerous ultraviolet radiation B. Excess ultraviolet radiation B can directly effect plant physiology and cause massive amounts of mutations, and indirectly through changed pollinator behavior, though such changes are simple to quantify. However, it has not yet been ascertained whether an increase in greenhouse gases would decrease stratospheric ozone levels.

In addition, a possible effect of rising temperatures is significantly higher levels of ground-level ozone, which would substantially lower yields.

ENSO Effects on Agriculture

ENSO (El Niño Southern Oscillation) will affect monsoon patterns more intensely in the future as climate change warms up the ocean's water. Crops that lie on the equatorial belt or under the tropical Walker circulation, such as rice, will be affected by varying monsoon patterns and more unpredictable weather. Scheduled planting and harvesting based on weather patterns will become less effective.

Areas such as Indonesia where the main crop consists of rice will be more vulnerable to the increased intensity of ENSO effects in the future of climate change. University of Washington professor, David Battisti, researched the effects of future ENSO patterns on the Indonesian rice agriculture using [IPCC]'s 2007 annual report and 20 different logistical models mapping out climate factors such as wind pressure, sea-level, and humidity, and found that rice harvest will experience a decrease in yield. Bali and Java, which holds 55 percent of the rice yields in Indonesia, will be likely to experience 9-10 percent probably of delayed monsoon patterns, which prolongs the hungry season. Normal planting of rice crops begin in October and harevest by January. However, as climate change affects ENSO and consequently delays planting, harvesting will be late and in drier conditions, resulting in less potential yields.

Impact of Agriculture on Climate Change

The agricultural sector is a driving force in the gas emissions and land use effects thought to cause climate change. In addition to being a significant user of land and consumer of fossil fuel, agriculture contributes directly to greenhouse gas emissions through practices such as rice production and the raising of livestock; according to the Intergovernmental Panel on Climate Change, the three main causes of the increase in greenhouse gases observed over the past 250 years have been fossil fuels, land use, and agriculture.

Land Use

Agriculture contributes to greenhouse gas increases through land use in four main ways:

- CO_2 releases linked to deforestation
- Methane releases from rice cultivation
- Methane releases from enteric fermentation in cattle
- Nitrous oxide releases from fertilizer application

Together, these agricultural processes comprise 54 percent of methane emissions, roughly 80 percent of nitrous oxide emissions, and virtually all carbon dioxide emissions tied to land use.

The planet's major changes to land cover since 1750 have resulted from deforestation in temperate regions: when forests and woodlands are cleared to make room for fields and pastures, the albedo of the affected area increases, which can result in either warming or cooling effects, depending on local conditions. Deforestation also affects regional carbon reuptake, which can result in increased concentrations of CO_2, the dominant greenhouse gas. Land-clearing methods such as slash and burn compound these effects by burning biomatter, which directly releases greenhouse gases and particulate matter such as soot into the air.

Livestock

Livestock and livestock-related activities such as deforestation and increasingly fuel-intensive farming practices are responsible for over 18 percent of human-made greenhouse gas emissions, including:

- 9 percent of global carbon dioxide emissions
- 35-40 percent of global methane emissions (chiefly due to enteric fermentation and manure)
- 64 percent of global nitrous oxide emissions (chiefly due to fertilizer use.

Livestock activities also contribute disproportionately to land-use effects, since crops such as corn and alfalfa are cultivated in order to feed the animals.

Worldwide, livestock production occupies 70 percent of all land used for agriculture, or 30 percent of the land surface of the Earth.

5
CHAPTER

RESPONSES TO GLOBAL WARMING

The broad agreement among climate scientists that global temperatures will continue to increase has led some nations, states, corporations and individuals to implement responses. These responses to global warming can be divided into mitigation of the causes and effects of global warming, adaptation to the changing global environment, and geoengineering to reverse global warming.

Mitigation

Carbon capture and storage (CCS) is an approach to mitigation. Emissions may be sequestered from fossil fuel power plants, or removed during processing in hydrogen production. When used on plants, it is known as bio-energy with carbon capture and storage.

The IPCC's Working Group III is responsible for crafting reports on mitigation of global warming and the costs and benefits of different approaches. The 2007 IPCC Fourth Assessment Report concludes that no one technology or sector can be completely responsible for mitigating future warming. They find there are key practices and technologies in various sectors, such as energy supply, transportation, industry, and agriculture that should be implemented to reduced global emissions. They estimate that stabilization of carbon dioxide equivalent between 445 and 710 ppm by 2030 will result in between a 0.6 percent increase and three percent decrease in global gross domestic product.

Mitigation of global warming is accomplished through reductions in the rate of anthropogenic greenhouse gas release. The world's primary international agreement on reducing greenhouse gas emissions, the Kyoto Protocol, now covers more than 160 countries and over 55 percent of global greenhouse gas emissions. As of February 2010, only the United States, historically the world's largest emitter of greenhouse gases, has refused to ratify the treaty. The treaty expires in 2012. International talks began in May 2007 on a future treaty to succeed the current one. The 2009 United Nations Climate Change Conference met in Copenhagen in December 2009 to agree on a framework for climate change mitigation. No binding agreement was made.

There has also been business action on climate change, including efforts to improve energy efficiency and limited moves towards use of alternative fuels. In January 2005 the European Union introduced its European Union Emission Trading Scheme, through which companies in conjunction with government agree to cap their emissions or to purchase credits from those below their allowances. Australia announced its Carbon Pollution Reduction Scheme in 2008. United States

President Barack Obama has announced plans to introduce an economy-wide cap and trade scheme.

Adaptation

A wide variety of measures have been suggested for adaptation to global warming, including: water conservation, water rationing, adaptive agricultural practices including diversification, construction of flood defenses, changes to medical care, and interventions to protect threatened species. The capacity and potential for human systems to adapt is unevenly distributed across different regions and populations. The economic costs of adaptation are potentially large, but also largely unknown. Across the literature, there is wide agreement that adaptation will be more difficult for larger magnitudes and higher rates of climate change.

Geoengineering

Geoengineering is the concept of planetary engineering applied to Earth: i.e. the deliberate modification of Earth's natural environment on a large scale to suit human needs. An example is greenhouse gas remediation, which removes greenhouse gases from the atmosphere, usually through carbon sequestration techniques such as carbon dioxide air capture. Solar radiation management reduces absorbed solar radiation, such as by the addition of stratospheric sulfur aerosols or cool roof techniques. No geoengineering projects of significant scale have been implemented, and detailed study has largely been the work of small numbers of scientists; but various significant institutions such as the Royal Society and IMechE have recently suggested that further study is warranted. Their various externalities and other costs are seen as major issues, and the idea or concern that one country could act unilaterally has also been raised.

Debate and Skepticism

Main articles: Global warming controversy and Politics of global warming

Increased publicity of the scientific findings surrounding global warming has resulted in political and economic debate. Poor regions, particularly Africa, appear at greatest risk from the projected effects of global warming, although their emissions have been small compared to those of the developed world. The exemption of developing countries from Kyoto Protocol restrictions has been used to justify non-ratification by the U.S. and a previous Australian Government. (Australia has since ratified the Kyoto protocol.) Another point of contention is the degree to which emerging economies such as India and China should be expected to constrain their emissions. The U.S. contends that if it must bear the cost of reducing emissions, then China should do the same[110][111] since China's gross national CO_2 emissions now exceed those of the U.S. China has contended that it is less obligated to reduce emissions since its per capita responsibility and per capita emissions are less that of the U.S. India, also exempt, has made similar contentions.

In 2007–2008 Gallup Polls surveyed 127 countries. Over a third of the world's population was unaware of global warming, with people in developing countries less aware than those in developed, and those in Africa the least aware. Of those aware, Latin America leads in belief that temperature changes are a result of human activities while Africa, parts of Asia and the Middle East, and a few countries from the Former Soviet Union lead in the opposite belief.[117] In the Western world, opinions over the concept and the appropriate responses are divided. Nick Pidgeon of Cardiff University finds that "results show the different stages of engagement about global warming on each side of the Atlantic"; where Europe debates the appropriate responses while the United States debates whether climate change is happening.

Debates weigh the benefits of limiting industrial emissions of greenhouse gases against the costs that such changes would entail. Using economic incentives, alternative and renewable energy have been promoted to reduce emissions while building infrastructure. Organizations such as the libertarian Competitive Enterprise Institute, conservative commentators, and companies such as ExxonMobil have challenged IPCC climate change scenarios, funded scientists who disagree with the scientific consensus, and provided their own projections of the economic cost of stricter controls. Environmental organizations and public figures have emphasized changes in the current climate and the risks they entail, while promoting adaptation to changes in infrastructural needs and emissions reductions. Some fossil fuel companies have scaled back their efforts in recent years, or called for policies to reduce global warming. Many studies link population growth with emissions and the effect of climate change.

Some global warming skeptics in the science or political communities dispute all or some of the global warming scientific consensus, questioning whether global warming is actually occurring, whether human activity has contributed significantly to the warming, and the magnitude of the threat posed by global warming.

6

CHAPTER

COPENHAGEN SUMMIT

The 2009 United Nations Climate Change Conference, commonly known as the Copenhagen Summit, was held at the Bella Center in Copenhagen, Denmark, between 7 December and 18 December. The conference included the 15th Conference of the Parties (COP 15) to the United Nations Framework Convention on Climate Change and the 5th Meeting of the Parties (COP/MOP 5) to the Kyoto Protocol. According to the Bali Road Map, a framework for climate change mitigation beyond 2012 was to be agreed there.

The conference was preceded by the Climate Change: Global Risks, Challenges and Decisions scientific conference, which took place in March 2009 and was also held at the Bella Center. The negotiations began to take a new format when in

May 2009 UN Secretary General Ban Ki-moon attended the World Business Summit on Climate Change in Copenhagen, organised by the Copenhagen Climate Council (COC), where he requested that COC councillors attend New York's Climate Week at the Summit on Climate Change on 22 September and engage with heads of government on the topic of the climate problem.

Connie Hedegaard was president of the conference until December 16, 2009, handing over the chair to Danish Prime Minister Lars Løkke Rasmussen in the final stretch of the conference, during negotiations between heads of state and government. On Friday 18 December, the final day of the conference, international media reported that the climate talks were "in disarray". Media also reported that in lieu of a summit collapse, solely a "weak political statement" was anticipated at the conclusion of the conference.

The Copenhagen Accord was drafted by the US, China, India, Brazil and South Africa on December 18, and judged a "meaningful agreement" by the United States government. It was "taken note of", but not "adopted", in a debate of all the participating countries the next day, and it was not passed unanimously. The document recognised that climate change is one of the greatest challenges of the present day and that actions should be taken to keep any temperature increases to below 2°C. The document is not legally binding and does not contain any legally binding commitments for reducing CO_2 emissions. Many countries and non-governmental organisations were opposed to this agreement, but, as of January 4, 2010, 138 countries have signed the agreement. Tony Tujan of the IBON Foundation suggests the perceived failure of Copenhagen may prove useful, if it allows people to unravel some of the underlying misconceptions and work towards a new, more holistic view of things. This could help gain the support of developing countries.

Negotiating Position of the European Union

On 28 January 2009, the European Commission released a position paper, "Towards a comprehensive climate agreement in Copenhagen."[11] The position paper "addresses three key challenges: targets and actions; financing [of "low-carbon development and adaptation"]; and building an effective global carbon market".

Leading by example, the European Union had committed to implementing binding legislation, even without a satisfactory deal in Copenhagen. Last December, the European Union revised its carbon allowances system called the Emissions Trading Scheme (ETS) designed for the post-Kyoto period (after 2013). This new stage of the system aims at further reducing greenhouse gases emitted in Europe in a binding way and at showing the commitments the EU had already done before the Copenhagen meeting. To avoid carbon leakage—relocation of companies in other regions not complying with similar legislation—the EU Commission will foresee that sectors exposed to international competition, should be granted some free allocations of CO_2 emissions provided that they are at least at the same level of a benchmark. Other sectors should buy such credits on an international market. Energy intensive industries in Europe have advocated for this benchmark system in order to keep funds in investment capacities for low carbon products rather than for speculations. The European chemical industry claims here the need to be closer to the needs of citizens in a sustainable way. To comply with such commitments for a low-carbon economy, this requires competitiveness and innovations.

The French Minister for Ecology Jean-Louis Borloo pushes the creation of the Global Environment Organisation as France's main institutional contribution, to offer a powerful alternative to the UNEP.

Official Pre-Copenhagen Negotiation Meetings

A draft negotiating text for finalisation at Copenhagen was publicly released. It was discussed at a series of meetings before Copenhagen.

Bonn – Second Negotiating Meeting

Delegates from 183 countries met in Bonn from 1 to 12 June 2009. The purpose was to discuss key negotiating texts. These served as the basis for the international climate change agreement at Copenhagen. At the conclusion the Ad Hoc Working Group under the Kyoto Protocol (AWG-KP) negotiating group was still far away from the emission reduction range that has been set out by science to avoid the worst ravages of climate change: a minus 25 percent to minus 40 percent reduction below 1990 levels by 2020. The AWG-KP still needs to decide on the aggregate emission reduction target for industrialised countries, along with individual targets for each country. Progress was made in gaining clarification of the issues of concern to parties and including these concerns in the updated draft of the negotiating text.

SEVENTH SESSION

Bangkok

The first part of the seventh session of the AWG-LCA was held in Bangkok, Thailand, from Monday, 28 September at the United Nations Conference Centre (UNCC) of the United Nations Economic and Social Commission for Asia and the Pacific (UNESCAP), Bangkok, Thailand.

Barcelona

The resumed session was held in Barcelona, Spain, from 2 to 6 November 2009. Thereafter, the AWG-LCA met to conclude its work at its eighth session, concurrently with the fifteenth session of the Conference of the Parties which opened in Copenhagen on 7 December 2009.

Listing of Proposed Actions

Proposed changes in absolute emissions		
Area	1990→2020	Reference base
Norway	−30% to −40%	CO_2e w/o LULUCF
Japan	−25%	
EU	−20 to −30%	CO_2e w/o LULUCF @ 20%
		CO_2e w/- LULUCF @ 30%
Russia	−20 to −25%	
South Africa	−18%	
Iceland	−15%	CO_2e w/- LULUCF
New Zealand	−10 to −20%	CO_2e w/- COP15 LULUCF
Australia	−4 to −24%	CO_2e w/o LULUCF
	−15 to −33%	CO_2e w/- human LULUCF
United States	−4%	CO_2e w/o LULUCF
Canada	−3%	CO_2e (LULUCF undecided)
Brazil	+5 to −1.8%	
Area	2005→2020	Reference base
China	−40 to −45% (per GDP)	CO_2 emissions intensity
India	−20 to −25% (per GDP)	CO_2e emissions intensity

During the conference some countries stated what actions they were proposing to take if a binding agreement was achieved. In the end, no such agreement was reached.

Australia

To cut carbon emissions by 25 percent below 2000 levels by 2020 if the world agrees to an ambitious global deal to stabilise levels of CO_2e to 450 ppm or lower.

To cut carbon emissions by 15 percent below 2000 levels by 2020 if there is an agreement where major developing economies commit to substantially restrain emissions and advanced economies take on commitments comparable to Australia.

To cut carbon emissions by 5 percent below 2000 levels by 2020 unconditionally.

It is clearly stated in proceedings from the Australian Senate and policy statements from the government that the Australian emission reductions include land use, land-use change and forestry (LULUCF) with the form of inclusion remaining undecided and whilst acknowledging that they are subject to the forming of accounting guidelines from this Copenhagen conference. In contention is the Australian Government's preference for the removal of non-human induced LULUCF emissions – and perhaps their abatement – from the account, such as from lightning induced bushfires and the subsequent natural carbon sequestering regrowth.

Using Kyoto accounting guidelines, these proposals are equivalent to an emissions cut of 24 percent, 14 percent and 4 percent below 1990 levels by 2020 respectively. Raw use of UNFCCC CO_2e data including LULUCF as defined during the conference by the UNFCCC for the years 2000 (404.392 Tg CO_2e) and 1990 (453.794 Tg CO_2e) leads to apparent emissions cuts of 33 percent (303.294 Tg CO_2e), 25 percent (343.733 Tg CO_2e) and 15 percent (384.172 Tg CO_2e) respectively.

Belarus

To reduce emissions by 5-10 percent below 1990 levels by 2020.

Brazil

To cut emissions by 38–42 percent below projected 2020 levels (if no action was taken) by the year 2020.

This is equivalent to a change to emissions to between 5 percent above and 1.8 percent below 1990 levels by 2020

Canada

To cut carbon emissions by 20 percent below 2006 levels by 2020. This is equivalent to 3 percent below 1990 levels by 2020.

The three most populous provinces disagree with the federal government goal and announced more ambitious targets on their jurisdictions. Quebec, Ontario and British Columbia announced respectively 20 percent, 15 percent and 14 percent reduction target below their 1990 levels while Alberta is expecting a 58 percent increase in emissions.

People's Republic of China

To cut CO_2 emissions intensity by 40–45% below 2005 levels by 2020.

Costa Rica

To become carbon neutral by 2021.

European Union

To cut greenhouse gas emissions by 30 percent (including LULUCF[21]) below 1990 levels by 2020 if an international agreement is reached committing other developed countries and the more advanced developing nations to comparable emission reductions.

To cut greenhouse gas emissions by 20 percent (excluding LULUCF) below 1990 levels by 2020 unconditionally.

Member country Germany has offered to reduce its CO_2 emissions by 40 percent below 1990 levels by 2020.

Iceland

To cut carbon emissions by 15 percent below 1990 levels by 2020.

India

To cut carbon emissions intensity by 20–25 percent below 2005 levels by 2020.

Indonesia

To reduce carbon emissions by 26 percent by 2020, based on business-as-usual levels. With enhanced international assistance, President of Indonesia Dr. Yudhoyono offered an increased reduction of 41 percent by 2020, based on business-as-usual levels.

Japan

To cut greenhouse gas emissions by 25 percent below 1990 levels by 2020.

Kazakhstan

To cut greenhouse gas emissions by 15 percent below 1992 levels by 2020.

Liechtenstein

To cut greenhouse gas emissions by 20-30 percent below 1990 levels by 2020.

Maldives

To become carbon neutral by 2019.

Mexico

To reduce emissions 50 percent by 2050 below 2000 levels.

Monaco

To cut greenhouse gas emissions by 20 percent below 1990 levels by 2020.

New Zealand

To reduce emissions between 10 percent to 20 percent below 1990 levels by 2020 if a global agreement is secured that limits carbon dioxide equivalent (CO_2e) to 450 ppm and temperature increases to 2°C, effective rules on forestry, and New Zealand having access to international carbon markets.

Norway

To reduce carbon emissions by 30 percent below 1990 levels by 2020.

During his speech at the conference, Prime Minister of Norway Jens Stoltenberg offered a 40 percent cut in emissions below 1990 levels by 2020 if it could contribute to an agreement.

Philippines

To reduce emissions 5 percent below 1990 levels.

Russia

Prior to the meeting, Russia pledged to reduce emissions between 20 percent to 25 percent below 1990 levels by 2020 if a global agreement is reached committing other countries to comparable emission reductions. This target had not been announced to the UNFCCC Secretariat before the COP 15 meeting. In the COP 15 negotiations, Russia only pledged to make a 10 percent to 15 percent reduction below 1990 levels by

2020 as part of a commitment to the Kyoto Protocol, but said that it would reduce emissions by 20 percent to 25 percent as part of an agreement on long-term cooperative action.

Singapore

To reduce emissions by 16 percent by 2020, based on business-as-usual levels.

South Africa

To cut emissions by 34 percent below current expected levels by 2020.

This is equivalent to an absolute emissions cut of about 18 percent below 1990 levels by 2020.

South Korea

To reduce emissions unilaterally by 4 percent below 2005 levels by 2020.

Switzerland

To reduce greenhouse gas emissions by 20-30 percent below 1990 levels by 2020.

Ukraine

To reduce greenhouse gas emissions by 20 percent below 1990 levels by 2020.

United States of America

To cut greenhouse gas emissions by 17 percent below 2005 levels by 2020, 42 percent by 2030 and 83 percent by 2050.

Raw use of UNFCCC CO_2e data excluding LULUCF as defined during the conference by the UNFCCC for the years 2005 (7802.213 Tg CO_2e and 1990 (6084.490 Tg CO_2e leads to apparent emissions cuts of about 4 percent (5878.24 Tg CO_2e), 33 percent (4107.68 Tg CO_2e) and 80 percent (1203.98 Tg CO_2e) respectively.

Technology Measures

UNEP

At the fifth Magdeburg Environmental Forum held from 3 to 4 July 2008, in Magdeburg, Germany, United Nations Environment Programme called for the establishment of infrastructure for electric vehicles. At this international conference, 250 high-ranking representatives from industry, science, politics and non-government organizations discussed solutions for future road transportation under the motto of "Sustainable Mobility– United Nations Climate Change Conference 2009|the Post-2012 CO_2 Agenda".

Technology Action Programs

Technology Action Programs (TAPs) have been proposed as a means for organizing future technology efforts under the UNFCCC. By creating programs for a set of adaptation and mitigation technologies, the UNFCCC would send clear signals to the private and finance sector, governments, research institutions as well as citizens of the world looking for solutions to the climate problem. Potential focus areas for TAPs include early warning systems, expansion of salinity-tolerant crops, electric vehicles, wind and solar energy, efficient energy grid systems, and other technologies.

Technology roadmaps will address barriers to technology transfer, cooperative actions on technologies and key economic sectors, and support implementation of Nationally Appropriate Mitigation Actions (NAMAs) and National Adaptation Programmes of Action (NAPAs).

Side Event on Technology Transfer

The United Nations Industrial Development Organisation (UNIDO) and the Department of Economic and Social Affairs (UNDESA) have been assigned the task of co-convening a process to support UN system-wide coherence and international cooperation on climate change-related technology development and transfer. This COP15 Side Event will feature statements and input from the heads of UNDESA, UNDP, GEF, WIPO, UNIDO, UNEP, IRENA as well as the UN Foundation. Relevant topics such as the following will be among the many issues discussed:

Technology Needs Assessments (TNA)

The Poznan Strategic Programme on Technology Transfer

UN-ENERGY

Regional Platforms and Renewable Energy Technologies

Related Public Actions

The Danish government and key industrial organizations have entered a public-private partnership to promote Danish cleantech solutions. The partnership, Climate Consortium Denmark, is an integrated part of the official portfolio of activities before, during and after the COP15.

There is also a European Conference for the Promotion of Local Actions to Combat Climate Change. The entire morning session on 25 September was devoted to the Covenant of Mayors.

The Local Government Climate Lounge will be an advocacy and meeting space located directly in the COP 15 building, at the heart of the negotiations.

THE CONFERENCE

Activism

Some small protests occurred during the first week of the conference. A much larger march was held in Copenhagen on December 12 calling for a global agreement on climate. Between 40,000 and 100,000 people attended. 968 protesters were detained at the event, including 19 who were arrested for carrying pocket knives and wearing masks during the demonstration. Of these all but 13 were released without charge. One police officer was injured by a rock and a protester was injured by fireworks. Some protestors were kettled by police and detained for several hours without access to food, water or toilets, before being arrested and taken to a holding facility on coaches. Protestors were said to be angry at the use of what they considered "heavy-handed" police tactics. Activists claimed that the police used wire-taps, undercover officers and pepper spray on people who had been detained. The police said the measures were necessary to deal with organisations such as Never Trust A COP which stated on its website that it would "consciously attack the structures supporting the COP15". Per Larsen, the chief coordinating officer for the Copenhagen police force told the *New York Times* that it was "surely the biggest police action we have ever had in Danish history."

The Yes Men made a false statement purporting to be from the Canadian environment minister Jim Prentice, which pledged to cut carbon emissions by 40 percent below 1990 levels by 2020. The statement was followed by another faked statement from the Ugandan delegation, praising the original pledge and The Yes Men also released a spoof press conference on a fake form of the official website. The statement was written about by the *Wall Street Journal* before being revealed as a hoax. Jim Prentice described the hoax as "undesirable".

Four Greenpeace activists gatecrashed a dinner that heads of states were attending on December 18. They unfurled banners saying "Politicians talk, leaders act" before being arrested. They were held without charge for almost three weeks and were not questioned by police until two weeks after their arrest.

International Activism

An estimated 20,000 people took part in a march held in London, one week before the conference started. They called on British leaders to force developed nations to cut their emissions by 40 percent by 2020 and to provide $150 billion a year by 2020 to assist the world's poorest countries in adapting to climate change.

As many as 50,000 people took part in a number of marches in Australia, during the conference, calling for world leaders to create a strong and binding agreement. The largest march took place in Melbourne.

Klimaforum09 - People's Climate Summit

Wahu Kaara (Global justice activist / Kenya Debt Relief Network) spoke at the closing ceremony at Klimaforum09 - People's Climate Summit in Copenhagen December 2009.

An alternative conference, Klimaforum09, was attended by about 50,000 people during the conference. Environmental activists from regions of the world most affected by climate change convened at Klimaforum09 with leaders such as Vandana Shiva, founder of Navdanya, and author Naomi Klein. A People's Declaration was formulated before and during the People's Climate Summit calling for "System change - not climate change" and handed over to the 15th Conference of the Parties at December 18.

The Danish Text

A leaked document known as "The Danish Text" has started an argument between developed and developing nations. The document was subtitled as "The Copenhagen Agreement" and proposes measures to keep average global temperature rises to two degrees Celsius above pre-industrial levels. Developing countries reacted to the document by saying that the developed countries had worked behind closed doors and made an agreement according to their wish without the consent of the developing nations. Lumumba Stanislaus Di-Aping, chairman of the G77, said, "It's an incredibly imbalanced text intended to subvert, absolutely and completely, two years of negotiations. It does not recognize the proposals and the voice of developing countries". A confidential analysis of the text by developing countries showed deep unease over details of the text.

Indigenous Rights

Indigenous rights organization Survival International has raised concerns that some measures to mitigate the problem of climate change affect the survival of tribal people as much as climate change. The United Nations Permanent Forum on Indigenous Issues has expressed similar concerns. Stephen Corry, director of Survival International, explains that "projects that victimise the people and harm the environment cannot be promoted or marketed as green projects". Survival International calls attention to the fact that these people, who least contribute to the problem of climate change, are already the most affected by it; and that we must seek solutions that involve indigenous people. Andrew E. Miller, human rights campaigner at Amazon Watch, said, "Many indigenous peoples, understandably, are skeptical that the latest silver bullet is really in their interest. In fact, serious concerns have arisen that implementation of REDD [Reducing Emissions from Deforestation and Forest

Degradation] could counteract fundamental indigenous rights, in the same way that countless conservation schemes have limited local subsistence activities and led to displacement around the world." Similar criticism came out of the climate justice network Climate Justice Now!

Negotiating Problems

On December 16, *The Guardian* reported that the summit in Copenhagen was in jeopardy. "We have made no progress" said a source close to the talks. "What people don't realise is that we are now not really ready for the leaders. These talks are now 17 hours late." Negotiators were openly talking of the best possible outcome being a "weak political agreement that would leave no clear way forward to tackle rising greenhouse gas emissions". This would mean that negotiations would continue into 2010 increasing the damage done by emissions.

On December 18, the head of the United Nations Environmental Program told the BBC that "the summit as of this morning is a summit in crisis" and that only the arrival of heads of state could bring the summit to a successful conclusion. Head of climate change for WWF in Britain, said that the proposals made so far, especially those from industrialised countries "all far short of what the world needs".

Hopenhagen

Hopenhagen is a climate change campaign organized by the United Nations and the International Advertising Association to support COP15, — the United Nations Climate Change Conference 2009. The creative council was chaired by Bob Isherwood and the ad agencies that created the campaign included Ogilvy & Mather, Euro RSCG, McCann Worldgroup, Draftfcb, Saatchi & Saatchi, Interbrand, Tribal DDB and Digitas. The campaign runs the web site http://www.

hopenhagen.org/ where users can sign a petition. Together with Huffington Post it also included sponsoring of a "Hopenhagen Ambassador", — a citizen journalist selected in a contest.

Renowned photographer John Clang has joined the global Hopenhagen effort with a stop-motion short film he created to bring awareness to the 2009 United Nations Climate Change Conference. In addition to the film, Clang shot and created a series of posters that bring to life the visual representation of Hopenhagen's citizens.

Outcome

On 18 December after a day of frantic negotiations between heads of state, it was announced that a "meaningful agreement" had been reached between on one hand the United States and on the other, in a united position as the BASIC countries, China, India, South Africa and Brazil. An unnamed US government official was reported as saying that the deal was a "historic step forward" but was not enough to prevent dangerous climate change in the future. However, the BBC's environment correspondent said: "While the White House was announcing the agreement, many other – perhaps most other – delegations had not even seen it. A comment from a UK official suggested the text was not yet final and the Bolivian delegation has already complained about the way it was reached – 'anti-democratic, anti-transparent and unacceptable'. With no firm target for limiting the global temperature rise, no commitment to a legal treaty and no target year for peaking emissions, countries most vulnerable to climate impacts have not got the deal they wanted."[100] The use of "meaningful" in the announcement was viewed as being political spin by an editorial in *The Guardian*.

Early on Saturday 19 December, delegates approved a motion to "take note of the Copenhagen Accord of December

18, 2009". This was due to the opposition of countries such as Bolivia, Venezuela, Sudan and Tuvalu who registered their opposition to both the targets and process by which the Copenhagen Accord was reached. The UN Secretary General Ban Ki-moon welcomed the US-backed climate deal as an "essential beginning" however debate has remained as to the exact legal nature of the Accord. The Copenhagen Accord recognises the scientific case for keeping temperature rises below 2°C, but does not contain commitments for reduced emissions that would be necessary to achieve that aim. One part of the agreement pledges US$ 30 billion to the developing world over the next three years, rising to US$100 billion per year by 2020, to help poor countries adapt to climate change. Earlier proposals, that would have aimed to limit temperature rises to 1.5°C and cut CO_2 emissions by 80 percent by 2050 were dropped. The Accord also favors developed countries' paying developing countries to reduce emissions from deforestation and degradation, known as "REDD". The agreement made was non-binding but US President Obama said that countries could show the world their achievements. He said that if they had waited for a binding agreement, no progress would have been made.

REACTIONS

Governments

US President Barack Obama said that the agreement would need to be built on in the future and that "We've come a long way but we have much further to go."

Prime Minister Gordon Brown of Great Britain said "We have made a start" but that the agreement needed to become legally binding quickly. He accused a small number of nations of holding the Copenhagen talks to ransom. EU Commission President Jose Manuel Barroso said "I will not hide my disappointment regarding the non-binding nature of the agreement here." French President Nicolas Sarkozy commented "The text we have is not perfect" however "If we had no deal, that would mean that two countries as important as India and China would be freed from any type of contract."

The head of China's delegation said that "The meeting has had a positive result, everyone should be happy." Wen Jiabao, China's prime minister said that the weak agreement was because of distrust between nations: "To meet the climate change challenge, the international community must strengthen confidence, build consensus, make vigorous efforts and enhance co-operation." India's environment minister, Jairam Ramesh, has been reported as saying, "We can be satisfied that we were able to get our way" and that India had "come out quite well in Copenhagen".

Brazil's climate change ambassador called the agreement "disappointing". The head of the G77 group of countries said that the draft text asked African countries to sign a "suicide pact" and that it would "maintain the economic dominance of a few countries". The values the solution was based on were "the very same values in our opinion that funnelled six million people in Europe into furnaces". Representatives of the Maldives, Venezuela, and Tuvalu were unhappy with the outcome. Bolivian president, Evo Morales said that, "The meeting has failed. It's unfortunate for the planet. The fault is with the lack of political will by a small group of countries led by the US."

John Ashe, the chair of the talks that led to the Kyoto protocol, was also disappointed with the agreement made, stating: "Given where we started and the expectations for this conference, anything less than a legally binding and agreed outcome falls far short of the mark."

Non-governmental Organizations

Rajendra K. Pachauri stated the Copenhagen Accord is "good but not adequate." John Sauven, executive director of Greenpeace UK stated that "The city of Copenhagen is a crime scene tonight ... It is now evident that beating global warming will require a radically different model of politics than the one on display here in Copenhagen." According to him "there are too few politicians in this world capable of looking beyond the horizon of their own narrow self-interest". Nnimmo Bassey, of Friends of the Earth international called the conference "an abject failure". Lydia Baker of Save the Children said that world leaders had "effectively signed a death warrant for many of the world's poorest children. Up to 250,000 children from poor communities could die before the next major meeting in Mexico at the end of next year." Tim Jones, climate policy officer from the World Development Movement said that leaders had "refused to lead and instead sought to bribe and bully developing nations to sign up to the equivalent of a death warrant."

Kim Carstensen of the World Wide Fund for Nature stated: "Well-meant but half-hearted pledges to protect our planet from dangerous climate change are simply not sufficient to address a crisis that calls for completely new ways of collaboration across rich and poor countries...We needed a treaty now and at best, we will be working on one in half a year's time. What we have after two years of negotiation is a half-baked text of unclear substance." Robert Bailey, of Oxfam International, said: "It is too late to save the summit, but it's not too late to save the planet and its people. We have no choice but to forge forward towards a legally binding deal in 2010. This must be a rapid, decisive and ambitious movement, not business as usual."

Analysis and Aftermath

Despite widely held expectations that the Copenhagen summit would produce a legally binding treaty, the conference was plagued by negotiating deadlock and the "Copenhagen Accord" is not legally enforceable. BBC environment analyst Roger Harrabin attributed the failure of the summit to live up to expectations to a number of factors including the recent global recession and conservative domestic pressure in the US and China.

In the week following the end of the Copenhagen summit, carbon prices in the EU dropped to a six month low.

The Copenhagen Accord asked countries to submit emissions targets by the end of January 2010, and paves the way for further discussions to occur at the 2010 UN climate change conference in Mexico and the mid-year session in Bonn. By early February, 67 countries had registered their targets. Countries such as India and Association of Island States made clear that they believed that Copenhagen Accord could not replace negotiations within the UNFCCC. Other commentators consider that "the future of the UN's role in international climate deals is now in doubt."

Failure Blamed on Developed Countries

George Monbiot blamed the failure of the conference to achieve a binding deal on the United States Senate and Barack Obama. By negotiating the Copenhagen Accord with only a select group of nations, most of the UN member states were excluded. If poorer nations did not sign the Accord then they would be unable to access funds from richer nations to help them adapt to climate change. He noted how the British and American governments have both blamed China for the failure of the talks but said that Obama placed China in "an impossible position" - "He demanded concessions while offering nothing." Martin Khor blamed Denmark for convening a meeting of only 26 nations in the final two days of the conference. He says that it undermined the UN's multilateral and democratic process of climate negotiations. It was in these meetings that China vetoed long-term emission-reduction goals for global emissions to decrease by 50 percent, and developed countries emissions to fall by 80 percent by 2050 compared to 1990. Khor states that this is when other countries began to blame the failures on China. If China had accepted this, by 2050 their emissions per capita would have had to be around one half to one fifth per capita of those of the United States.

Failure Blamed on Developing Countries

The Australian Broadcasting Corporation has reported that India, China and other emerging nations cooperated at Copenhagen to thwart attempts at establishing legally binding targets for carbon emissions, in order to protect their economic growth.

UK Climate Change secretary Ed Miliband accused China specifically of sinking an agreement, provoking a counter response from China that British politicians were engaging in a political scheme. Mark Lynas, who was attached to the Maldives delegation, accused China of "sabotaging" the talks and ensuring that Barack Obama would publicly shoulder the blame. The New York Times has quoted Lynas as further commenting:

> "...the NGO movement is ten years out of date. They're still arguing for 'climate justice', whatever that means, which is interpreted by the big developing countries like India and China as a right to pollute up to Western levels. To me carbon equity is the logic of mutually assured destruction. I think NGOs are far too soft on the Chinese, given that it's the world's biggest polluter, and is the sin-

> gle most important factor in deciding when global emissions will peak, which in turn is the single most important factor in the eventual temperature outcome...
>
> "I think the bottom line for China (and India) is growth, and given that this growth is mainly based on coal, there is going to have to be much more pressure on China if global emissions are to peak within any reasonable time frame. In Beijing the interests of the Party come first, second and third, and global warming is somewhere further down the list. Growth delivers stability and prosperity, and keeps the party in power."

China's Xinhua news agency responded to these allegations by asserting that Premier Wen Jiabao played a sincere, determined and constructive role at the last minute talks in Copenhagen and credited him with playing a key role in the "success" of the conference. However, Wen did not take part in critical closed-door discussions at the end of the conference. According to Wen himself, the Chinese delegation was not informed about the critical discussion.

The editorial of News Corporation's *The Australian* newspaper, blamed African countries for turning Copenhagen into "a platform for demands that the world improve the continent's standard of living" and claimed that "Copenhagen was about old-fashioned anti-Americanism, not the environment".

Indian journalist Praful Bidwai puts the blame on both developed and a few developing countries such as India, arguing that the "Copenhagen Accord is an illegitimate, ill-conceived, collusive deal between a handful of countries that are some of the world's greatest present and future emitters." He argues that India's policy is driven by elites determined to maintain high-consumer lifestyles which will have devastating effects for the vast majority of India's poor.

Academics

In a panel discussion held at MIT, Henry Jacoby gave the results of an analysis on the effect of the commitments made in the Accord. According to this analysis, assuming that the commitments submitted in response to the Accord (as of February 2010) are fulfilled, global emissions would peak around 2020. The resultant stock of emissions was projected to exceed the level required to have a roughly 50 percent chance of meeting the 2 °C target that is specified in the Accord. In his assessment, even emission reductions below that needed to reach the 2 °C target had the benefit of reducing the risk of large amounts of future climate change.

Benito Müller commented on criticisms of the UNFCCC process. In his view, the failure to get a better result at Copenhagen was due to a lack of political will in the months preceding the conference.

7
CHAPTER

KYOTO PROTOCOL

The Kyoto Protocol is a protocol to the United Nations Framework Convention on Climate Change (UNFCCC or FCCC), aimed at fighting global warming. The UNFCCC is an international environmental treaty with the goal of achieving "stabilization of greenhouse gas concentrations in the atmosphere at a level that would prevent dangerous anthropogenic interference with the climate system."

The Protocol was initially adopted on 11 December 1997 in Kyoto, Japan and entered into force on 16 February 2005. As of November 2009, 187 states have signed and ratified the protocol.

Under the Protocol, 37 industrialized countries (called "Annex I countries") commit themselves to a reduction of four greenhouse gases (GHG) (carbon dioxide, methane, nitrous oxide, sulphur hexafluoride) and two groups of gases (hydrofluorocarbons and perfluorocarbons) produced by them, and all member countries give general commitments. Annex I countries agreed to reduce their collective greenhouse gas emissions by 5.2 percent from the 1990 level. Emission limits do not include emissions by international aviation and shipping, but are in addition to the industrial gases, chlorofluorocarbons, or CFCs, which are dealt with under the 1987 Montreal Protocol on Substances that Deplete the Ozone Layer.

The benchmark 1990 emission levels were accepted by the Conference of the Parties of UNFCCC (decision 2/CP.3) were the values of "global warming potential" calculated for the IPCC Second Assessment Report. These figures are used for converting the various greenhouse gas emissions into comparable CO_2 equivalents when computing overall sources and sinks.

The Protocol allows for several "flexible mechanisms", such as emissions trading, the clean development mechanism (CDM) and joint implementation to allow Annex I countries to meet their GHG emission limitations by purchasing GHG emission reductions credits from elsewhere, through financial exchanges, projects that reduce emissions in non-Annex I countries, from other Annex I countries, or from annex I countries with excess allowances.

Each Annex I country is required to submit an annual report of inventories of all anthropogenic greenhouse gas emissions from sources and removals from sinks under UNFCCC and the Kyoto Protocol. These countries nominate a person (called a "designated national authority") to create and manage its greenhouse gas inventory. Virtually all of the non-Annex I countries have also established a designated national authority to manage its Kyoto obligations, specifically the

"CDM process" that determines which GHG projects they wish to propose for accreditation by the CDM Executive Board.

Background

The view that human activities are likely responsible for most of the observed increase in global mean temperature ("global warming") since the mid-20th century is an accurate reflection of current scientific thinking (NRC, 2001, p. 3, 2008, p. 2). Human-induced warming of the climate is expected to continue through the 21st century.

IPCC (2007) produced a range of projections of what the future increase in global mean temperature might be. Projections spanned a range due to socio-economic uncertainties, e.g., over future greenhouse gas (GHG) emission levels, and uncertainties with regard to physical science aspects, e.g., the climate sensitivity. For the time period 2090-2099, measured from global mean temperature in the period 1980-1999, the "likely" range (as assessed to have a greater than 66 percent probability of being correct, based on expert judgment) across the six SRES "marker" emissions scenarios was projected as an increase in global mean temperature of 1.1 to 6.4 °C.

The scientific question of what constitutes a "safe" level of atmospheric greenhouse gas concentrations has been asked (NRC, 2001, p. 4). This question cannot be answered directly since it requires value judgments of, for example, what would be an acceptable risk to human welfare. In general, however, risks increase with both the rate and magnitude of future climate change

Ratification Process

The Protocol was adopted by COP 3 on 11 December 1997 in Kyoto, Japan. It was opened on 16 March 1998 for signature by parties to UNFCCC.

Countries which are parties to UNFCCC [show]

Afghanistan (non-party to Kyoto)	Dominican Republic	Lithuania	Saudi Arabia
Albania	Ecuador	Luxembourg	Senegal
Algeria	Egypt	Republic of Macedonia	Serbia
Angola	El Salvador	Madagascar	Seychelles
Antigua and Barbuda	Equatorial Guinea	Malawi	Sierra Leone
Argentina	Eritrea	Malaysia	Singapore
Armenia	Estonia	Maldives	Slovakia
Australia	Ethiopia	Mali	Slovenia
Austria	European Union	Malta	Solomon Islands
Azerbaijan	Fiji	Marshall Islands	South Africa
Bahamas	Finland	Mauritania	Spain
Bahrain	France	Mauritius	Sri Lanka
Bangladesh	Gabon	Mexico	Sudan
Barbados	Gambia	Federated States of Micronesia	Suriname
Belarus	Georgia	Moldova	Swaziland
Belgium	Germany	Monaco	Sweden
Belize	Ghana	Mongolia	Switzerland
Benin	Greece	Montenegro	Syria
Bhutan	Grenada	Morocco	Tajikistan
Bolivia	Guatemala	Mozambique	Tanzania
Bosnia and Herzegovina	Guinea	Namibia	Thailand
Botswana	Guinea-Bissau	Nauru	Timor-Leste
Brazil	Guyana	Nepal	Togo
Brunei	Haiti	Netherlands	Tom
Bulgaria	Honduras	New Zealand	Tonga
Burkina Faso	Hungary	Nicaragua	Trinidad and Tobago
Myanmar	Iceland	Niger	Tunisia
Burundi	India	Nigeria	Turkey
Cambodia	Indonesia	Niue	Turkmenistan
Cameroon	Iran	Norway	Tuvalu
Canada	Ireland	Oman	Uganda
Cape Verde	Israel	Pakistan	Ukraine
Central African Republic	Italy	Palau	United Arab Emirates
Chad	Jamaica	Panama	United Kingdom
Chile	Japan	Papua New Guinea	United States (non-party to Kyoto)
China	Jordan	Paraguay	Uruguay
Colombia	Kazakhstan	Peru	Uzbekistan
Comoros	Kenya	Philippines	Vanuatu
Democratic Republic of the Congo	Kiribati	Poland	Venezuela
Republic of the Congo	North Korea	Portugal	Vietnam
Cook Islands	South Korea	Qatar	Yemen
Costa Rica	Kuwait		
	Kyrgyzstan		

<table>
<tr>
<td>Côte d'Ivoire
Croatia
Cuba
Cyprus
Czech Republic
Denmark
Djibouti
Dominica</td>
<td>Laos
Latvia
Lebanon
Lesotho
Liberia
Libya
Liechtenstein</td>
<td>Romania
Russia
Rwanda
Saint Kitts and Nevis
Saint Lucia
Saint Vincent and the Grenadines
Samoa
San Marino (non-party to Kyoto)
São Tomé and Príncipe</td>
<td>Zambia
Zimbabwe
• Observers:
Andorra (non-party to Kyoto) Holy See (non-party to Kyoto) Iraq
Somalia (non-party to Kyoto)</td>
</tr>
</table>

Article 25 of the Protocol specifies that the Protocol enters into force "on the ninetieth day after the date on which not less than 55 Parties to the Convention, incorporating Parties included in Annex I which accounted in total for at least 55 percent of the total carbon dioxide emissions for 1990 of the Annex I countries, have deposited their instruments of ratification, acceptance, approval or accession."

The EU and its Member States ratified the Protocol in May 2002. Of the two conditions, the "55 parties" clause was reached on 23 May 2002 when Iceland ratified the Protocol. The ratification by Russia on 18 November 2004 satisfied the "55%" clause and brought the treaty into force, effective 16 February 2005, after the required lapse of 90 days.

As of November 2009, 186 countries and one regional economic organization (the EC) have ratified the agreement, representing over 63.9% of the 1990 emissions from Annex I countries. The most notable non-party to the Protocol is the United States, which is a party to UNFCCC and was responsible for 36.1 percent of the 1990 emission levels of Annex I countries. The Protocol can be signed and ratified only by parties to UNFCCC, (Article 24) and a country can withdraw by giving 12 months notice. (Article 27)

Objectives

The objective is the "stabilization and reconstruction of greenhouse gas concentrations in the atmosphere at a level that would prevent dangerous anthropogenic interference with the climate system."

The objective of the Kyoto climate change conference was to establish a legally binding international agreement, whereby all the participating nations commit themselves to tackling the issue of global warming and greenhouse gas emissions. The target agreed upon was an average reduction of 5.2% from 1990 levels by the year 2012. According to the treaty, in 2012, Annex I countries must have fulfilled their obligations of reduction of greenhouse gases emissions established for the first commitment period (2008–2012).

The five principal concepts of the Kyoto Protocol are:

- commitments to reduce greenhouse gases that are legally binding for annex I countries, as well as general commitments for all member countries;
- implementation to meet the Protocol objectives, to prepare policies and measures which reduce greenhouse gases; increasing absorption of these gases (for example through geosequestration and biosequestration) and use all mechanisms available, such as joint implementation, clean development mechanism and emissions trading; being rewarded with credits which allow more greenhouse gas emissions at home;
- minimizing impacts on developing countries by establishing an adaptation fund for climate change;
- accounting, reporting and review to ensure the integrity of the Protocol;

- compliance by establishing a compliance committee to enforce commitment to the Protocol.

2012 Emission Targets and "Flexible Mechanisms"

Thirty-nine of the 40 Annex I countries have ratified the Protocol. Of these 34 have committed themselves to a reduction of greenhouse gases (GHG) produced by them to targets that are set in relation to their 1990 emission levels, in accordance with Annex B of the Protocol. The targets apply to the four greenhouse gases carbon dioxide, methane, nitrous oxide, sulphur hexafluoride, and two groups of gases, hydrofluorocarbons and perfluorocarbons. The six GHG are translated into CO_2 equivalents in determining reductions in emissions. These reduction targets are in addition to the industrial gases, chlorofluorocarbons, or CFCs, which are dealt with under the 1987 Montreal Protocol on Substances that Deplete the Ozone Layer.

Under the Protocol, Annex I countries have committed themselves to national or joint reduction targets, (formally called "quantified emission limitation and reduction objectives"- Article 4.1) that range from a joint reduction of 8 percent for the European Union and others, to 7 percent for the United States (non-binding as the US is not a signatory), 6 percent for Japan and 0 percent for Russia. The treaty permits emission increases of 8 percent for Australia and 10 percent for Iceland. Emission limits do not include emissions by international aviation and shipping.

Annex I countries under the Kyoto Protocol, their 2012 commitments (% of 1990) and 1990 emission levels (% of all Annex I countries) [show]

Australia – 108% (2.1% of 1990 emissions) Austria – 92% (0.4%) Belarus – 95% (subject to acceptance by other parties) Belgium – 92% (0.8%) Bulgaria – 92% (0.6%) Canada – 94% (3.33%) Croatia – 95% () Czech Republic – 92% (1.24%) Denmark – 92% (0.4%) Estonia – 92% (0.28%)	Finland – 92% (0.4%) France – 92% (2.7%) Germany – 92% (7.4%) Greece – 92% (0.6%) Hungary – 94% (0.52%) Iceland – 110% (0.02%) Ireland – 92% (0.2%) Italy – 92% (3.1%) Japan – 94% (8.55%) Latvia – 92% (0.17%)	Liechtenstein – (0.0015%) 92% Lithuania – 92% () Luxembourg – 92% (0.1%) Monaco – 92% (0.0015%) Netherlands – 92% (1.2%) New Zealand – 100% (0.19%) Norway – 101% (0.26%) Poland – 94% (3.02%) Portugal – 92% (0.3%) Romania – 92% (1.24%)	Russian Federation – 100% (17.4%) Slovakia – 92% (0.42%) Slovenia – 92% () Spain – 92% (1.9%) Sweden – 92% (0.4%) Switzerland – 92% (0.32%) Turkey () Ukraine – 100% () United Kingdom – 92% (4.3%) United States of America – 93% (36.1%) (non-party)

Annex I countries can achieve their targets by allocating reduced annual allowances to major operators within their borders, or by allowing these operators to exceed their allocations by offsetting any excess through a mechanism that is agreed by all the parties to the UNFCCC, such as by buying emission allowances from other operators which have excess emissions credits.

Thirty-eight of the 39 Annex I countries have agreed to cap their emissions in this way, two others are required to do so under their conditions of accession into the EU, and one more (Belarus) is seeking to become an Annex I country.

Flexible Mechanisms

The Protocol defines three "flexibility mechanisms" that can be used by Annex I countries in meeting their emission reduction commitments (Bashmakov *et al.*, 2001, p. 402). The flexibility mechanisms are International Emissions Trading (IET), the Clean Development Mechanism (CDM), and Joint Implementation (JI). IET allows Annex I countries to "trade" their emissions (Assigned Amount Units, AAUs, or "allowances" for short). For IET, the economic basis for providing this flexibility is that the marginal cost of emission abatement differs among countries. Trade could potentially allow the Annex I countries to meet their emission reduction commitments at a reduced cost. This is because trade allows emissions to be abated first in countries where the costs of abatement are lowest, thus increasing the efficiency of the Kyoto agreement.

The CDM and JI are called "project-based mechanisms," in that they generate emission reductions from projects. The difference between IET and the project-based mechanisms is that IET is based on the setting of a quantitative restriction of emissions, while the CDM and JI are based on the idea of "production" of emission reductions (Toth *et al.*, 2001, p. 660). The CDM is designed to encourage production of emission reductions in non-Annex I countries, while JI encourages production of emission reductions in Annex I countries.

The production of emission reductions generated by the CDM and JI can be used by Annex B countries in meeting their emission reduction commitments. The emission reductions produced by the CDM and JI are both measured against a hypothetical baseline of emissions that would have occurred in the absence of a particular emission reduction project. The emission reductions produced by the CDM are called "Certified Emission Reductions" (CERs); reductions produced by JI are called "Emission Reduction Units" (ERUs). The reductions are called "credits" because they are emission reductions credited against a hypothetical baseline of emissions.

International Emissions Trading

The most advanced emissions trading system (ETS) is the one developed by the EU (Gupta *et al.*, 2007). Ellerman and Buchner (2008) (referenced in Grubb *et al.*, 2009, p. 11) suggested that during its first two years in operation, the EU ETS turned an expected increase in emissions of 1-2 percent per year into a small absolute decline. Grubb *et al.* (2009, p. 11) suggested that a reasonable estimate for the emissions cut achieved during its first two years of operation was 50-100 $MtCO_2$ per year, or 2.5-5 percent.

Clean Development Mechanism

Between 2001, which was the first year CDM projects could be registered, and 2012, the end of the Kyoto commitment period, the CDM is expected to produce some 1.5 billion tons of carbon dioxide equivalent (CO_2e) in emission reductions. Most of these reductions are through renewable energy, energy efficiency, and fuel switching (World Bank, 2010, p. 262). By 2012, the largest potential for production of CERs are estimated in China (52% of total CERs) and India (16%). CERs produced in Latin America and the Caribbean make up 15 percent of the potential total, with Brazil as the largest producer in the region (7%).

Joint Implementation

The formal crediting period for JI was aligned with the first commitment period of the Kyoto Protocol, and did not start until January 2008 (Carbon Trust, 2009, p. 20). In November 2008, only 22 JI project had been officially approved and registered. The total projected emission savings from JI by 2012 are about one tenth that of the CDM. Russia accounts for about two-thirds of these savings, with the remainder divided up roughly equally between the Ukraine and the EU's New

Member States. Emission savings include cuts in methane, HFC, and N_2O emissions.

Details of the Agreement

According to a press release from the United Nations Environment Program:

> "After 10 days of tough negotiations, ministers and other high-level officials from 160 countries reached agreement this morning on a legally binding Protocol under which industrialized countries will reduce their collective emissions of greenhouse gases by 5.2 percent. The agreement aims to lower overall emissions from a group of six greenhouse gases by 2008–12, calculated as an average over these five years. Cuts in the three most important gases – carbon dioxide (CO_2), methane (CH_4), and nitrous oxide (N_2O) – will be measured against a base year of 1990. Cuts in three long-lived industrial gases – hydrofluorocarbons (HFCs), perfluorocarbons (PFCs), and sulphur hexafluoride (SF6) – can be measured against either a 1990 or 1995 baseline."

National limitations range from 8 percent reductions for the European Union and others, to 7 percent for the US, 6 percent for Japan, 0 percent for Russia, and permitted increases of 8 percent for Australia and 10 percent for Iceland.

The agreement supplements the United Nations Framework Convention on Climate Change (UNFCCC) adopted at the Earth Summit in Rio de Janeiro in 1992, which did not set any limitations or enforcement mechanisms. All parties to UNFCCC can sign or ratify the Kyoto Protocol, while non-parties to UNFCCC cannot. The Kyoto Protocol was adopted at the third session of the Conference of Parties to the UNFCCC (COP 3) in 1997 in Kyoto, Japan. Most provisions of the Kyoto Protocol apply to developed countries, listed in Annex I to UNFCCC.

National emission targets exclude international aviation and shipping.

Common but Differentiated Responsibility

UNFCCC adopts a principle of "common but differentiated responsibilities." The parties agreed that:

1. the largest share of historical and current global emissions of greenhouse gases originated in developed countries;
2. per capita emissions in developing countries are still relatively low; and
3. the share of global emissions originating in developing countries will grow to meet social and development needs.

Emissions

Per-capita emissions are a country's total emissions divided by its population (Banuri *et al.*, 1996, p. 95). Per-capita emissions in the industrialized countries are typically as much as ten times the average in developing countries (Grubb, 2003, p. 144). This is one of the reasons why industrialized countries accepted responsibility for leading climate change efforts in the Kyoto negotiations. In Kyoto, the countries that took on quantified commitments for the first period (2008–12) corresponded roughly to those with per-capita emissions in 1990 of two tonnes of carbon or higher. In 2005, the top-20 emitters comprised 80 percent of total GHG emissions (PBL, 2010. See also the notes in the following section on the top-ten emitters in 2005). Countries with a Kyoto target made up 20 percent of total GHG emissions.

Another way of measuring GHG emissions is to measure the total emissions that have accumulated in the atmosphere over time (IEA, 2007, p. 199). Over a long time period, cumulative emissions provide an indication of a country's total contribution to GHG concentrations in the atmosphere.

Over the 1900-2005 period, the US was the world's largest cumulative emitter of energy-related CO_2 emissions, and accounted for 30 percent of total cumulative emissions (IEA, 2007, p. 201). The second largest emitter was the EU, at 23 percent; the third largest was China, at 8 percent; fourth was Japan, at 4 percent; fifth was India, at 2 percent. The rest of the world accounted for 33 percent of global, cumulative, energy-related CO_2 emissions.

Top Ten Emitters

What follows is a ranking of the world's top ten emitters of GHGs for 2005 (MNP, 2007). The first figure is the country's or region's emissions as a percentage of the global total. The second figure is the country's/region's per-capita emissions, in units of tons of GHG per-capita:

1. China – 17%, 5.8
2. United States ® – 16%, 24.1
3. European Union-27 ® – 11%, 10.6
4. Indonesia - 6%, 12.9
5. India – 5%, 2.1
6. Russia ® – 5%, 14.9
7. Brazil – 4%, 10.0
8. Japan ® – 3%, 10.6
9. Canada ® – 2%, 23.2
10. Mexico – 2%, 6.4

Notes

- These values are for the GHG emissions from fossil fuel use and cement production. Calculations are for carbon dioxide (CO_2), methane (CH_4), nitrous oxide

(N_2O) and fluor containing gases (the F-gases HFCs, PFCs and SF_6).

- These estimates are subject to large uncertainties regarding CO_2 emissions from deforestation; and the per country emissions of other GHGs (e.g., methane). There are also other large uncertainties which mean that small differences between countries are not significant. CO_2 emissions from the decay of remaining biomass after biomass burning/deforestation are not included.
- *Industrialised countries*: official country data reported to UNFCCC (®)
- [1] excluding underground fires.[2] including an estimate of 2000 million tonnes CO_2 from peat fires and decomposition of peat soils after draining. However, the uncertainty range is very large.

Financial Commitments

The Protocol also reaffirms the principle that developed countries have to pay billions of dollars, and supply technology to other countries for climate-related studies and projects. The principle was originally agreed in UNFCCC.

Revisions

The protocol left several issues open to be decided later by the sixth Conference of Parties (COP). COP6 attempted to resolve these issues at its meeting in the Hague in late 2000, but was unable to reach an agreement due to disputes between the European Union on the one hand (which favoured a tougher agreement) and the United States, Canada, Japan and Australia on the other (which wanted the agreement to be less demanding and more flexible).

In 2001, a continuation of the previous meeting (COP6bis) was held in Bonn where the required decisions were adopted. After some concessions, the supporters of the protocol (led by the European Union) managed to get Japan and Russia in as well by allowing more use of carbon dioxide sinks.

COP7 was held from 29 October 2001 through 9 November 2001 in Marrakech to establish the final details of the protocol.

The first Meeting of the Parties to the Kyoto Protocol (MOP1) was held in Montreal from 28 November to 9 December 2005, along with the 11th conference of the Parties to the UNFCCC (COP11).

The 3 December 2007, Australia ratified the protocol during the first day of the COP13 in Bali.

Of the signatories, 36 developed C.G. countries (plus the EU as a party in the European Union)agreed to a 10 percent emissions increase for Iceland; but, since the EU's member states each have individual obligations, much larger increases (up to 27%) are allowed for some of the less developed EU countries). Reduction limitations expire in 2013.

Enforcement

If the enforcement branch determines that an annex I country is not in compliance with its emissions limitation, then that country is required to make up the difference plus an additional 30 percent. In addition, that country will be suspended from making transfers under an emissions trading program.

Negotiations

Article 4.2 of the UNFCCC commits industrialized countries to "[take] the lead" in reducing emissions (Grubb, 2003, p. 144). The initial aim was for industrialized countries to stabilize their emissions at 1990 levels by the year 2000. The failure of key industrialized countries to move in this direction was a principal reason why Kyoto moved to binding commitments.

At the first UNFCCC Conference of the Parties in Berlin, the G77 (a coalition of 77 developing nations within the UN) was able to push for a mandate where it was recognized that (Liverman, 2008, p. 12):

- developed nations had contributed most to the then-current concentrations of GHGs in the atmosphere;
- developing country emissions per-capita were still relatively low; and
- that the share of global emissions from developing countries would grow to meet their development needs.

This mandate was recognized in the Kyoto Protocol in that developing countries were not subject to emission reduction commitments in the first Kyoto commitment period. However, the large potential for growth in developing country emissions made negotiations on this issue tense (Grubb, 2003, p. 145-146). In the final agreement, the Clean Development Mechanism was designed to limit emissions in developing countries, but in such a way that developing countries do not bear the costs for limiting emissions. The general assumption was that developing countries would face quantitative commitments in later commitment periods, and at the same time, developed countries would meet their first round commitments.

Base Year

The choice of the 1990 base year remains in Kyoto, as it does in the original Framework Convention. The desire to move to historical emissions was rejected on the basis that good data was not available prior to 1990. The 1990 base year also favoured several powerful interests including the UK, Germany and Russia (Liverman, 2008, p. 12). This is because the UK and Germany had high CO_2 emissions in 1990.

In the UK following 1990, emissions had declined because of a switch from coal to gas ("dash for gas"), which has lower emissions than coal. This was due to the UK's privatization of coal mining and its switch to natural gas supported by North sea reserves. Germany benefitted from the 1990 base year because of its reunification between West and East Germany. East Germany's emissions fell dramatically following the collapse of East German industry after the fall of the Berlin Wall. Germany could therefore take credit for the resultant decline in emissions.

Japan promoted the idea of flexible baselines, and favoured a base year of 1995 for HFCs. Their HFC emissions had grown in the early 1990s as a substitute for CFCs banned in the Montreal Protocol (Liverman, 2008, p. 13). Some of the former Soviet satellites wanted a base year to reflect their highest emissions prior to their industrial collapse.

Emissions Cuts

The G77 wanted strong uniform emission cuts across the developed world of 15 percent (Liverman, 2008, p. 13). Countries, such as the US, made suggestions to reduce their responsibility to reduce emissions. These suggestions included:

- The inclusion of carbon sinks (e.g., by including forests, that absorb CO_2 from the atmosphere).
- And having net current emissions as the basis for responsibility, i.e., ignoring historical emissions.

The US originally proposed for the second round of negotiations on Kyoto commitments to follow the negotiations of the first (Grubb, 2003, p. 148). In the end, negotiations on the second period were set to open no later than 2005. Countries over-achieving in their first period commitments can "bank" their unused allowances for use in the subsequent period.

The EU initially argued for only three GHGs to be included – CO_2, CH_4, and N_2O – with other gases such as HFCs regulated separately (Liverman, 2008, p. 13). The EU also wanted to have a "bubble" commitment, whereby it could make a collective commitment that allowed some EU members to increase their emissions, while others cut theirs. The most vulnerable nations – the Association of Small Island States (AOSIS) – pushed for deep uniform cuts by developed nations, with the goal of having emissions reduced to the greatest possible extent.

The final days of negotiation of the Protocol saw a clash between the EU and the US and Japan (Grubb, 2003, p. 149). The EU aimed for flat-rate reductions in the range of 10-15 percent below 1990 levels, while the US and Japan supported reductions of 0-5 percent. Countries that had supported differentiation had different ideas as to how it should be calculated, and many different indicators were proposed: relating to GDP, energy intensity (energy use per unit of economic output), etc. According to Grubb (2003, p. 149), the only common theme of these indicators was that each proposal suited the interests of the country making the proposal.

The final commitments negotiated in the Protocol are the result of last minute political compromises (Liverman, 2008, p. 13-14). These include an 8 percent cut from the 1990 base year for the EU, 7 percent for the US, 6 percent for Canada and Japan, no cut for Russia, and an 8 percent increase for Australia. This sums to an overall cut of 5.2 percent below 1990 levels. Since Australia and the US did not ratify the treaty (although Australia has since done), the cut is reduced from 5.2 percent to about 2 percent.

Considering the growth of some economies and the collapse of others since 1990, the range of implicit targets is much greater (Aldy *et al.*, 2003, p. 7). The US faced a cut of about 30 percent below "business-as-usual" (BAU) emissions (i.e., predicted emissions should their be no attempt to limit emissions), while Russia and other economies in transition faced targets that allowed substantial increases in their emissions above BAU. On the other hand, Grubb (2003, p. 151) pointed out that the US, having per-capita emissions twice that of most other OECD countries, was vulnerable to the suggestion that it had huge potential for making reductions. From this viewpoint, the US was obliged to cut emissions back more than other countries.

Flexibility Mechanisms

Negotiations over the flexibility mechanisms included in the Protocol proved controversial (Grubb, 2003, p. 153). Japan and some EU member states wanted to ensure that any emissions trading would be competitive and transparent. Their intention was to prevent the US from using its political leverage to gain preferential access to the likely surplus in Russian emission allowances. The EU was also anxious to prevent the US from avoiding domestic action to reduce its emissions. Developing countries were concerned that the US would use flexibility to its own advantage, over the interests of weaker countries.

Compliance

The protocol defines a mechanism of "compliance" as a "monitoring compliance with the commitments and penalties for non-compliance." According to Grubb (2003, p. 157), the explicit consequences of non-compliance of the treaty are weak compared to domestic law. Yet, the compliance section of the treaty was highly contested in the Marrakesh Accords.

According to Grubb (2003), Japan made some unsuccessful efforts to "water-down" the compliance package.

Current Positions of Governments

ANNEX I

Australia

On the change of government following the election in November 2007, Prime Minister Kevin Rudd signed the ratification immediately after assuming office on 3 December 2007, just before the meeting of the UN Framework Convention on Climate Change; it took effect in March, 2008. According the Australian government, Australia should meet its Kyoto target (IEA, 2005, p. 56; DCCEE, 2010).

Canada

On 17 December 2002, Canada ratified the treaty that came into force in February 2005 (IEA, 2004, p. 52). In the assessment of NRTEE (2008), "Canada is not pursuing a policy objective of meeting the Kyoto Protocol emissions reductions targets. [...] [The] projected emissions profile described in the 2008 [government plan] would leave Canada in non-compliance with the Kyoto Protocol."

Europe

On 31 May 2002, all fifteen then-members of the European Union deposited the relevant ratification paperwork at the UN. All but one EU Member State (Austria) anticipate that they will meet their commitments under the Kyoto Protocol (EEA, 2009, pp. 11-12).

Norway

Between 1990 and 2007, Norway's greenhouse gas emissions increased by 12 percent. As well as directly reducing their own greenhouse gas emissions, Norway's idea for carbon neutrality is to finance reforestation in China, a legal provision of the Kyoto protocol.

Japan

Japan's emission reduction commitment under Kyoto is to reduce emissions by 6 percent on 1990 levels (Stern, 2007, p. 456). Japan had a national objective to increase its share of electricity from renewable sources to 20 percent by 2010.

Russia

Vladimir Putin approved the treaty on 4 November 2004, and Russia officially notified the United Nations of its ratification on 18 November 2004. The issue of Russian ratification was particularly closely watched in the international community, as the accord was brought into force 90 days after Russian ratification (16 February 2005).

The Kyoto Protocol limits emissions to a percentage increase or decrease from their 1990 levels. Since 1990, the economies of most countries in the former Soviet Union have collapsed, as have their greenhouse gas emissions. Because of this, Russia should have no problem meeting its commitments under Kyoto, as its current emission levels are substantially below its limitations.

United States

The United States (U.S.), although a signatory to the Kyoto Protocol, has neither ratified nor withdrawn from the Protocol. The signature alone is merely symbolic, as the Kyoto Protocol is non-binding on the United States unless ratified.

The US has a federal objective to reduce its GHG intensity level by 18 percent on 2002 levels by 2012 (Stern, 2007, p.

456). States have their own policies to cut emissions, including California, and states in the North-East and mid-Atlantic.

The North-East and Mid-Atlantic States are adhering to the new RGGI (Regional Greenhouse Gas Initiative) policy.

Non-Annex I

The CDM has been the mechanism by which non-Annex I countries have participated in the Kyoto Protocol. Many Non-Annex I countries already have policies in place to reduce greenhouse gas emissions, e.g., taxes, renewable energy and energy efficiency goals, but these are not recognized as climate change commitments in the Protocol (Stern, 2007, p. 478).

Brazil

Brazil has a national objective to increase the share of alternative renewable energy sources (biomass, wind and small hydropower) to 10 percent by 2030. It also has programmes to protect public forests from deforestation (Stern, 2007, p. 456).

People's Republic of China

A report by the Carbon Trust (2009) assessed the use of the CDM in China. The CDM has been used to finance projects in China for renewable energy and HFC-23 reductions (HFC's are powerful greenhouse gases). For renewables, the CDM was judged to have helped to stimulate wind and small hydro power projects. Critics have argued that these policies would generally have taken place without the CDM (Carbon Trust, 2009, p. 56).

The Chinese 11th Five Year Plan has a number of stringent national objectives to reduce emissions, one of which is a 20 percent reduction in energy intensity of GDP, from 2005 to 2010 (Stern, 2007, p. 456). According to World Bank (2010, p. 192), this target, if met, will reduce annual CO_2 emissions by

1.5 billion tons in 2010. This is the most aggressive emission reduction target in the world, and is five times larger than the EU's Kyoto emission reduction commitment, and eight times larger than California's target.

India

India signed and ratified the Protocol in August, 2002. Since India is exempted from the framework of the treaty, it is expected to gain from the protocol in terms of transfer of technology and related foreign investments.

Policies in India related to greenhouse gas emissions have included the 11th Five Year Plan, that contains mandatory and voluntary measures to increase efficiency in power generation and distribution. Other measures include increased use of nuclear power and renewable energy (Stern, 2007, p. 456).

Pakistan

On 11 January 2005, Pakistan submitted its instruments of accession to the Kyoto Protocol. In February, 2006, the national CDM operational strategy was approved, and on 27 April 2006, the first CDM project was approved by DNA. It was reduction of large N_2O from nitric acid production (investor: Mitsubishi, Japan), estimating 1 million CERs annually. In November, 2006, the first CDM project was registered with the United Nations Framework Convention on Climate Change (UNFCCC).

Views on the Protocol

Gupta *et al.*. (2007) assessed the literature on climate change policy. They found that no authoritative assessments of the UNFCCC or its Protocol asserted that these agreements had, or will, succeed in solving the climate problem. In these assessments, it was assumed that the UNFCCC or its Protocol would not be changed. The Framework Convention and its Protocol include provisions for future policy actions to be taken.

World Bank (2010, p. 233) commented on how the Kyoto Protocol had only had a slight effect on curbing global emissions growth. The treaty was negotiated in 1997, but by 2005, energy-related emissions had grown 24 percent. World Bank (2010) also stated that the treaty had provided only limited financial support to developing countries to assist them in reducing their emissions and adapting to climate change.

Some of the criticism of the Protocol has been based on the idea of climate justice (Liverman, 2008, p. 14). This has particularly centred on the balance between the low emissions and high vulnerability of the developing world to climate change, compared to high emissions in the developed world.

Some environmentalists have supported the Kyoto Protocol because it is "the only game in town," and possibly because they expect that future emission reduction commitments may demand more stringent emission reductions (Aldy *et al.*., 2003, p. 9). In 2001, sixteen national science academies stated that ratification of the Protocol represented a "small but essential first step towards stabilising atmospheric concentrations of greenhouse gases." Some environmentalists and scientists have criticized the existing commitments for being too weak (Grubb, 2000, p. 5).

Many economists think that the commitments are stronger than is justified (Grubb, 2000, p. 31). The lack of quantitative emission commitments for developing countries led the US and Australia (under Prime Minister John Howard) to decide not to ratify the treaty (Stern 2007, p. 478). Australia, under Prime Minister Kevin Rudd, has since ratified the treaty.

Change in Greenhouse Gas Emission since 1990

Progress toward the emission reduction commitments set in the Kyoto Protocol has been mixed. World Bank (2008, p. 6) reported that there were significant differences in performance across individual countries:

- For the Annex I non-Economies-in-Transition (non-EIT) Kyoto Protocol (KP) Parties, emissions in 2005 were 5 percent higher than 1990 levels (World Bank, 2008, p. 59). Their Kyoto target for 2008-2012 is for a 6 percent reduction in emissions. The Annex I non-EITs KP Parties are Australia, Austria, Belgium, Canada, Denmark, Finland, France, Germany, Greece, Iceland, Ireland, Italy, Japan, Liechtenstein, Luxembourg, Monaco, Netherlands, New Zealand, Norway, Portugal, Spain, Sweden, Switzerland, and the United Kingdom.
- The Annex I Economies in Transition (EIT) KP Parties emissions in 2005 were 35 percent below 1990 levels. Their Kyoto target is for a 2 percent reduction. The Annex I EIT KP Parties are Belarus, Bulgaria, Croatia, Czech Republic, Estonia, Hungary, Latvia, Lithuania, Poland, Romania, Russian Federation, Slovakia, Slovenia, and Ukraine.
- In 2005, the Annex I non-KP Parties emissions were 18 percent above their 1990 levels. The Annex I non-KP Parties are Turkey and the United States.
- In total, the Annex I KP Parties emissions for 2005 were 14 percent below their 1990 levels. Their Kyoto target is for a 4 percent reduction.

Annex I

KP Parties

According to the Netherlands Environmental Assessment Agency (PBL, 2009), the industrialized countries with a Kyoto target will, as a group, probably meet their emission limitation requirements. Collectively, this was for a 4 percent reduction relative to 1990 levels. A linear extrapolation of the 2000-2005 emissions trend led to a projected emission reduction in 2010 of almost 11 percent. Including the potential contribution of CDM projects, which may account for emissions reductions of approximately 500 megatonnes CO_2-eq per year, the reduction might be as large as 15 percent.

The expected reduction of 11 percent was attributed to the limited increase in emissions in OECD countries, but was particularly due to the large reduction of about 40 percent until 1999 in the EITs. The reduction in emissions for the smaller EITs aids the EU-27 in meeting their collective target. The EU expects that it will meet its collective target of an 8 percent reduction for the EU-15. This reduction includes:

- CDM and JI projects, which are planned to contribute 2.5 percent towards the target;
- Carbon storage in forests and soils (carbon sinks), which contribute another 0.9 percent.

Japan expects to meet its Kyoto target, which includes a 1.6 percent reduction from CDM projects and a 3.9 percent reduction from carbon storage, contributing to a total reduction of 5.5 percent. In other OECD countries, emissions have increased. In Canada, Australia, New Zealand and Switzerland, emissions have increased by 25 percent compared to the base year, while in Norway, the increase was 9 percent. In the view of PBL (2009), these countries will only be able to meet their targets by purchasing sufficient CDM credits or by buying emissions ("hot air") from EIT countries.

Non KP-Parties

Emissions in the US have increased 16 percent since 1990. According to PBL (2009), the US will not meet its original Kyoto target of a 6 percent reduction in emissions.

Non-Annex I

In several large developing countries and fast growing economies (China, India, Thailand, Indonesia, Egypt, and Iran) GHG emissions have increased rapidly (PBL, 2009). For example, emissions in China have risen strongly over the 1990-2005 period, often by more than 10 percent per year. Emissions per-capita in non-Annex I countries are still, for the most part, much lower than in industrialized countries. Non-Annex I countries do not have quantitative emission reduction commitments, but they are committed to mitigation actions. China, for example, has had a national policy programme to reduce emissions growth, which included the closure of old, less efficient coal-fired power plants.

8

CHAPTER

POST-KYOTO PROTOCOL NEGOTIATIONS ON GREENHOUSE GAS EMISSIONS

Post-Kyoto negotiations refers to high level talks attempting to address global warming by limiting greenhouse gas emissions. Generally part of the United Nations Framework Convention on Climate Change (UNFCCC), these talks concern the period after the first "commitment period" of the Kyoto Protocol, which is due to expire at the end of 2012. Negotiations have been mandated by the adoption of the Bali Roadmap and Decision 1/CP.13 ("The Bali Action Plan").

UNFCCC negotiations are conducted within two subsidiary bodies, the Ad Hoc Working Group on Long-term Cooperative Action under the Convention (AWG-LCA) and the Ad Hoc Working Group on Further Commitments for Annex I

Parties under the Kyoto Protocol (AWG-KP) and are expected to culminate in the United Nations Climate Change Conference taking place in December 2009 in Copenhagen (COP-15); negotiations are supported by a number of external processes, including the G8 process, a number of regional meetings and the Major Economies Forum on Energy and Climate that was launched by US President Barack Obama in March 2009. High level talks were held at the meeting of the G8+5 Climate Change Dialogue in February 2007 and at a number of subsequent G8 meetings, most recently leading to the adoption of the G8 leaders declaration "Responsible Leadership for a Sustainable Future" during the G8 summit in L'Aquila, Italy, in July 2009.

February 2007 Washington Declaration

In the non-binding "Washington Declaration" on February 16, 2007, the G8+5 group of leaders agreed in principle to a global cap-and-trade system that would apply to both industrialized nations and developing countries, which they hoped would be in place by 2009.

33rd G8 Summit

On June 7, 2007, leaders at the 33rd G8 summit issued a non-binding communiqué announcing that the G8 nations would "aim to at least halve global CO_2 emissions by 2050". The details enabling this to be achieved would be negotiated by environment ministers within the United Nations Framework Convention on Climate Change in a process that would also include the major emerging economies. Groups of countries would also be able to reach additional agreements on achieving the goal outside and in parallel with the United Nations process. The G8 also announced their desire to use the proceeds from the auction of emission rights and other financial tools to support climate protection projects in developing countries.

The agreement was welcomed by British Prime Minister Tony Blair as "a major, major step forward". French president Nicolas Sarkozy would have preferred a binding figure for emissions reduction to have been set. This was apparently blocked by U.S. President George W. Bush until the other major greenhouse gas emitting countries, like India and China, make similar commitments.

2007 UN General Assembly Plenary Debate

As part of the schedule leading up to the September UN High-Level-Event, on July 31 the United Nations General Assembly opened its first-ever plenary session devoted exclusively to climate change, which also included prominent scientists and business leaders. The debate, at which nearly 100 nations spoke, was scheduled to last two days but was extended for a further day to allow a greater number of "worried nations" to describe their climate-related problems.

In his opening speech, Secretary-General Ban Ki-moon urged Member States to work together, stating that the time had come for "decisive action on a global scale", and called for a "comprehensive agreement under the United Nations Framework Convention on Climate Change process that tackles climate change on all fronts, including adaptation, mitigation, clean technologies, deforestation and resource mobilization". In closing the conference General Assembly President Haya Rashed Al-Khalifa called for an "equitable, fair and ambitious global deal to match the scale of the challenges ahead". She had earlier stressed the urgency of the situation, stating that "the longer we wait, the more expensive this will be".

The day after the session ended, the UN launched its new climate change web site detailing its activities relating to global warming.

2007 Vienna Climate Change Talks and Agreement

A round of climate change talks under the auspices of the United Nations Framework Convention on Climate Change (UNFCCC) concluded in Austria in 31 August 2007 with agreement on key elements for an effective international response to climate change.

A key feature of the talks was a United Nations report that showed how energy efficiency could yield significant cuts in emissions at low cost.

The talks set the stage for the 2007 United Nations Climate Change Conference held in Bali in December 2007.

September 2007 United Nations High-Level-Event

As well as the meeting of the United Nations General Assembly, Secretary-General Ban Ki-moon was to hold informal high-level discussions on the post-Kyoto treaty on September 24. It was expected that these would pave the way for the United Nations Climate Change Conference, held in Bali in December 2007. Three Special Envoys on Climate Change, appointed on May 1, 2007, held discussions with various governments to define and plan the event.

In advance of the "High-Level-Event", the Secretary-General hoped that world leaders would "send a powerful political signal to the negotiations in Bali that "business as usual" will not do and that they are ready to work jointly with others towards a comprehensive multilateral framework for action".

September 2007 Washington Conference

It emerged on August 3, 2007, that representatives of the United Nations, major industrialized and developing countries are being invited by George Bush to a conference in Washington on September 27 and 28. Countries invited are believed to include the members of the G8+5 (Canada, France, Germany, Italy, Japan, Russia, United Kingdom, United States, Brazil, China, India, Mexico and South Africa), together with South Korea, Australia, Indonesia and South Africa. The meeting is to be hosted by US Secretary of State Condoleezza Rice, and is envisaged as the first of several extending into 2008. Initial reaction to the news of the conference invitation was mixed.

2007 United Nations Climate Change Conference in Bali

Negotiations on a successor to the Kyoto Protocol dominated the 2007 United Nations Climate Change Conference conference. A meeting of environment ministers and experts held in June called on the conference to agree a road-map, timetable and "concrete steps for the negotiations" with a view to reaching an agreement by 2009.

2008 United Nations Climate Change Conference in Poznań

Following preliminary talks in Bangkok, Bonn, and Accra,[21] the 2008 negotiations culminated in December with the 2008 United Nations Climate Change Conference in Poznań, Poland.

September 2009 United Nations Secretary General's Summit on Climate Change

United Nations Secretary General Ban Ki-Moon convened a high-level event on Climate Change on 22 September 2009 to which Heads of State and Government have been invited. This event was intended to build further political momentum for an ambitious Copenhagen agreed outcome to be adopted at COP-15.

2009 United Nations Climate Change Conference in Copenhagen (COP-15)

Following preparatory talks in Bonn, Bangkok and

Barcelona, the 2009 conference was held in December 2009 in Copenhagen, Denmark, and the treaty succeeding the Kyoto Protocol had been expected to be adopted there.

Some media sources claimed beforehand that the meeting would lead to empty promises without measurable goals. In a meeting of the Group of Eight G8, the world top leaders agreed to halve carbon emissions by 2050; however, they did not set specific targets because they did not agree on a base year. However members of the climate council acknowledged that action needs to happen fast. "My personal view is that the future of humanity is at stake," said Tim Flannery, Professor at Macquaire University and chairman of the Copenhagen Climate Council, in an interview with chinadialogue.net.

At the Conference, delegates approved a motion to "take note of the Copenhagen Accord of December 18, 2009". However it was reported that it was not yet clear whether the motion was unanimous, or what its legal implications are. The UN Secretary General Ban Ki-moon welcomed the US-backed climate deal as an "essential beginning". It was unclear whether all 192 countries in attendance would also adopt the deal. The Copenhagen Accord recognises the scientific case for keeping temperature rises below 2°C, but does not contain commitments for reduced emissions that would be necessary to achieve that aim. One part of the agreement pledges US$ 30 billion to the developing world over the next three years, rising to US$ 100 billion per year by 2020, to help poor countries adapt to climate change. Earlier proposals, that would have aimed to limit temperature rises to 1.5°C and cut CO_2 emissions by 80 percent by 2050 were dropped. An agreement was also reached that would set up a deal to reduce deforestation in return for cash from developed countries.

GLOSSARY

A

- **Albedo** - An index of the "reflectiveness" - a way of quantifying how much radiation is reflected back, as opposed to that absorbed.
- **Anoxic event** - a period when the Earth's oceans are free of oxygen below the surface layer.
- **Antarctic oscillation** (AAO) - a low-frequency mode of atmospheric variability of the southern hemisphere.
- **Anthropogenic** - literally, man-made.
- **Anthropogenic climate change** - climate change with the presumption of human influence, usually warming.

- **Anthropogenic global warming** (AGW) – global warming with the presumption of human influence.
- **Anti-greenhouse effect** - the cooling effect an atmosphere has on the ambient temperature of the planet.
- **Arctic amplification** - The effect of sea ice melting replace high albedo ice with low albedo sea that absorb the radiation from the sun get warmer and melt more ice.
- **Arctic oscillation** (AO) - the dominant pattern of non-seasonal sea-level pressure (SLP) variations north of 20 degrees N, and it is characterized by SLP anomalies of one sign in the Arctic and anomalies of opposite sign centered about 37-45 degrees N. See also NAO.
- **Arctic shrinkage** - the marked decrease in Arctic sea ice and the observed melting of the Greenland Ice Sheet in recent years.
- **Atlantic Multidecadal Oscillation** (AMO) - a hypothesised mode of natural variability occurring in the North Atlantic Ocean and which has its principle expression in the sea surface temperature (SST) field.
- **Atmospheric sciences** - an umbrella term for the study of the atmosphere, its processes, the effects other systems have on the atmosphere, and the effects of the atmosphere on these other systems.
- **Atmospheric window** - refers to those parts of the electromagnetic spectrum that are, with the Earth's atmosphere in its natural state, not absorbed at all.
- **Attribution of recent climate change** - the study of the causes of climate change.

B

- **Black carbon** - an aerosol or particulate (see also radiative forcing).

C

- **Carbon cycle** - the biogeochemical cycle by which carbon is exchanged between the biosphere, geosphere, hydrosphere, and atmosphere of the Earth.
- **Carbon diet** - the act of reducing the output of CO_2 to reduce impact on the environment.
- **Carbon sequestration** - proposals for removing CO_2 from the atmosphere, or for preventing CO_2 from fossil fuel use ever being released.
- **Carbon offset** - opportunity for individuals and businesses to neutralize their contribution to climate change.
- **Carbon tax** - a tax on energy sources which emit carbon dioxide.
- **Clathrate gun hypothesis** - the hypothesis that melting methance clathrates could trigger runaway or very severe global warming.
- **Climate** - the average and variations of weather in a region over long periods of time.
- **Climate change** - changes of climate in general, usually with no presumption of human influence. Note, however, that there is one important exception to this: the UNFCCC defines "climate change" as anthropogenic.
- **Climate commitment** - how much future warming is "committed", even if greenhouse gas levels do not rise.

- **Climate ethics** - an area of research that focuses on the ethical dimensions of climate change.
- **Climate legislation** - legislation dealing with regulation of greenhouse gas emissions.
- **Climate refugee** - a displaced person caused by climate change induced environmental disasters.
- **Climate variability** - climate change, with no presumption of cause.
- **Climatology** (Climate Science) - the study of climate, scientifically defined as weather conditions averaged over a period of time.

D

- Desertification - the degradation of land in arid and dry sub-humid areas, resulting primarily from natural activities and influenced by climatic variations
- **Detection and attribution** - see attribution of recent climate change

E

- **Eco-efficiency** - creating more goods and services while using fewer resources and creating less waste and pollution.
- **Earth's atmosphere** - a layer of gases surrounding the planet Earth and retained by the Earth's gravity.
- **Earthshine** - sunlight reflected from Earth and illuminating the dark side of the Moon.
- **Ecotax** - fiscal policy that introduces taxes intended to promote ecologically sustainable activities via economic incentives.

- **El Niño-Southern Oscillation** (ENSO) - a set of specific interacting parts of a single global system of coupled ocean-atmosphere climate fluctuations that come about as a consequence of oceanic and atmospheric circulation.
- **Emission standards** - requirements that set specific limits to the amount of pollutants that can be released into the environment
- **Enteric fermentation** - fermentation that takes place in the digestive systems of ruminant animals.
- **Environmental crime** - crime against environmental legislation that is liable for prosecution.

F

- **Feedbacks** - either an amplification (**positive feedback**) or a reduction (**negative feedback**) of the rate of global warming caused by its effects.
- **Fossil fuel** - fossil source fuels, that is, hydrocarbons found within the top layer of the earth's crust.
- **Freon** - DuPont's trade name for its odorless, colorless, nonflammable, and noncorrosive chlorofluorocarbon and hydrochlorofluorocarbon refrigerants, which are used in air conditioning and refrigeration systems.

G

- **Glacial earthquake** -large scale tremblors that occur in glaciated areas where the glacier moves faster than one kilometer per year.
- **Global cooling** - conjecture during the 1970s of imminent cooling of the Earth's surface and atmosphere along with a posited commencement of glaciation.

- **Global climate model**, also **General Circulation Model** or **GCM** - a computer model of the world's climate system, including the atmosphere and oceans.
- **Global dimming** - the observed decrease in surface insolation, that may have recently reversed
- **Global warming** (GW) - usually: the warming trend over the past century or so; also: any period in which the temperature of the Earth's atmosphere increases; also the theory of such changes.
- **Global warming controversy** - socio-political issues surrounding the theory of global warming.
- **Global warming period** - any period in which the temperature of the Earth's atmosphere increases
- **Global warming potential** - a measure of how much a given mass of greenhouse gas is estimated to contribute to global warming.
- **Greenhouse effect** - both natural and anthropogenic
- **Greenhouse gas** - gasses that cause the greenhouse effect
- **Gulf Stream** - a powerful, warm, and swift Atlantic ocean current that originates in the Gulf of Mexico, exits through the Strait of Florida, and follows the eastern coastlines of the United States and Newfoundland before crossing the Atlantic Ocean.

H

- **Heiligendamm Process** - an initiative that will institutionalize high level dialogue between the G8 countries and the five most important emerging economies, known as the O5 (Outreach 5) composed of China, Mexico, India, Brazil and South Africa; and the establishment of a common G5 + G8 platform at the OECD.

- **Historical temperature record** - see temperature record.
- **Hockey stick controversy** - a dispute over the reconstructed estimates of Northern Hemisphere mean temperature changes over the past millennium, frequently referred to as the MBH98 reconstruction.
- **Holocene** - a geological period, which began approximately 11,550 calendar years BP (about 9600 BC) and continued to the Anthropocene.
- **Holocene Climatic Optimum** - a warm period during roughly the interval 9,000 to 5,000 years B.P.

I

- **Ice age** - a period of long-term reduction in the temperature of Earth's climate, resulting in an expansion of the continental ice sheets, polar ice sheets and alpine glaciers.
- **Ice core** - a core sample from the accumulation of snow and ice over many years that have re-crystallized and have trapped air bubbles from previous time periods.
- **Insolation** - amount of solar radiation reaching the surface of the Earth.
- **Irradiance** - amount of electromagnetic radiation reaching a surface, measured in watts per square meter.
- **Instrumental temperature record** - shows the fluctuations of the temperature of the atmosphere and the oceans as measured by temperature sensors. The longest-running quasi-global record starts in 1850.

- **Interdecadal Pacific Oscillation** (IPO) - a cycle of 15–30 years between warm or cool waters in the north and south Pacific.

K

- **Kyoto Protocol** - modification to UNFCCC. See also Post-Kyoto Protocol negotiations on greenhouse gas emissions

L

- **Little Ice Age** - a period of cooling occurring after a warmer era known as the Medieval climate optimum.

M

- **Magnetosphere** - the region around an astronomical object in which phenomena are dominated or organized by its magnetic field.
- **Maunder Minimum** - the name given to the period roughly from 1645 to 1715, when sunspots became exceedingly rare, as noted by solar observers of the time.
- **Mauna Loa** - home to the longest instrumental CO_2 record.
- **Medieval climate optimum** - warm period from about the 10th century to about the 14th century.
- **Meteorology** - the interdisciplinary scientific study of the atmosphere that focuses on weather processes and forecasting.
- **Methane** - a greenhouse gas released by enteric fermentation in livestock, rice production, and fossil fuel extraction.

- **Mitigation of global warming** - involves taking actions to reduce greenhouse gas emissions and to enhance sinks aimed at reducing the extent of global warming
- **Mode of variability** - a pattern of climate change, usually oscillatory, with specific regional effects

N

- **Nitrous oxide** (N_2O) - a potent greenhouse gas produced primarily in agriculture, particularly by the livestock sector.
- **North Atlantic Deep Water** - one of the water masses of the ocean
- **North Atlantic oscillation** - an atmospheric climate mode

O

- **Ocean planet** - the opposite concept of Snowball Earth.
- **Ozone depletion** - not strongly connected to climate change

P

- **Pacific decadal oscillation** (PDO) - a 23-year pattern of warm or cool water in the north Pacific.
- **Paleocene–Eocene Thermal Maximum** (PETM) - a sudden warming event that fundamentally altered geological and biological aspects of the planet.
- **Paleoclimatology** - the study of climate change taken on the scale of the entire history of Earth.
- **Polar amplification** - greater temperature increases in the *Arctic* than in the earth as a whole) is a result of the

collective effect of feedbacks and other processes."[1] It does not apply to the Antarctic, because the Southern Ocean acts as a heat sink.[2]

- **Polar city** - a proposed human refuge located in northern regions of the Earth, and in Tasmania, New Zealand and the Antarctica, where people might have to live in order to survive major global warming "events" in the far distant future, also dubbed Lovelock Retreats.
- **Proxy** - a variable that can be related to one of interest (e.g. tree rings can be proxies for temperature variations).

R

- **Radiative forcing** - is (loosely) defined as the change in net irradiance at the tropopause
- **Runaway greenhouse effect** - somewhat ill-defined term, associated with the idea of large irreversible temperature rises

S

- **Slash and burn** - form of deforestation used to clear fields for agricultural use.
- **Solar variation** - changes in the amount of radiant energy emitted by the Sun.
- **Sunspot** - a region on the Sun's surface (photosphere) that is marked by a lower temperature than its surroundings and has intense magnetic activity, which inhibits convection, forming areas of low surface temperature. Sunspot activity is subject to research on climate change.

T

- **Thermohaline circulation** - the global density-driven circulation of the oceans.
- **TEX-86** - a paleothermometer based on the composition of membrane lipids of the marine picoplankton *Crenarchaeota*.
- **Thermocline** - (sometimes metalimnion) is a layer within a body of water or air where the temperature changes rapidly with depth.
- **Tipping point (climatology)** - the point at which change due to human activity brings about sufficient new processes in nature to make any human reversal of the change impossible.
- ***The Real Global Warming Disaster** - a 2009 book by Christopher Booker that examines skeptically the subject of man made global warming.

U

- **Urban heat island** - a metropolitan area which is significantly warmer than its surroundings.

BIBLIOGRAPHY

Association of British Insurers (June 2005). *Financial Risks of Climate Change* (PDF).

Ammann, Caspar; et al. (2007). "Solar influence on climate during the past millennium: Results from transient simulations with the NCAR Climate Simulation Model". Proceedings of the National Academy of Sciences of the United States of America. ***104*** (10): 3713–3718.

Barnett, TP; Adam, JC; Lettenmaier, DP (17 November 2005). "Potential impacts of a warming climate on water availability in snow-dominated regions", Nature. ***438*** (7066): 303–309.

Behrenfeld, MJ; O'malley, RT; Siegel, DA; et al. (7 December 2006). "Climate-driven trends in contemporary ocean productivity". Nature. ***444*** (7120): 752–755.

Choi, Onelack; Fisher, Ann (May 2005). "The Impacts of Socioeconomic Development and Climate Change on Severe Weather Catastrophe Losses: Mid-Atlantic Region (MAR) and the U.S". Climate Change. ***58*** (1–2): 149–170.

Dyurgerov, Mark B.; Meier, Mark F. (2005). *Glaciers and the Changing Earth System: a 2004 Snapshot.* Institute of Arctic and Alpine Research Occasional Paper #58.

Emanuel, KA (4 August 2005). "Increasing destructiveness of tropical cyclones over the past 30 years". Nature. ***436*** (7051): 686–688.

James E. Hansen; Larissa Nazarenko; Reto Ruedy; Makiko Sato; Josh Willis; Anthony Del Genio; Dorothy Koch; Andrew Lacis; Ken Lo; Surabi Menon; Tica Novakov; Judith Perlwitz; Gary Russell; Gavin A. Schmidt; Nicholas Tausnev (3 June 2005). "Earth's Energy Imbalance: Confirmation and Implications". Science. ***308*** (5727): 1431–1435.

Hinrichs, Kai-Uwe; Hmelo, Laura R.; Sylva, Sean P. (21 February 2003). "Molecular Fossil Record of Elevated Methane Levels in Late Pleistocene Coastal Waters". Science. ***299*** (5610): 1214–1217.

Hirsch, Tim (11 January 2006). "Plants revealed as methane source". BBC.

Hoyt, Douglas V.; Schatten, Kenneth H. (November 1993). "A discussion of plausible solar irradiance variations, 1700–1992". Journal of Geophysical Research. ***98*** (A11): 18,895–18,906.

IPCC TAR SYR (2001). Watson, R. T.; the Core Writing Team, eds. *Climate Change 2001: Synthesis Report.* Contribution of Working Groups I, II, and III to the *Third Assessment Report* of the Intergovernmental Panel on Climate Change. Cambridge University Press

Ivanova, Diana; Stadler, Konstantin; Steen-Olsen, Kjartan; Wood, Richard; Vita, Gibran; Tukker, Arnold; Hertwich, Edgar G. (18 December 2015). "Environmental Impact Assessment of Household Consumption". *Journal of Industrial Ecology*. ***20*** (3): 526–536.

Jamet, S.; J. Corfee-Morlot (7 April 2009). *"Assessing the Impacts of Climate Change: A Literature Review"*. OECD Economics Department Working Papers. OECD (691). *doi:10.1787/224864018517*.. Paper at IDEAS.

Karnaukhov, A. V. (2001). "Role of the Biosphere in the Formation of the Earth's Climate: The Greenhouse Catastrophe". Biophysics. ***46*** (6).

Kenneth, James P. (14 February 2003). *Methane Hydrates in Quaternary Climate Change: The Clathrate Gun Hypothesis*. American Geophysical Union.

Keppler, Frank; et al. (18 January 2006). *Global Warming – The Blame Is not with the Plants*. Max Planck Society.

Lean, Judith L.; Wang, Y.M.; Sheeley, N.R. (December 2002). "The effect of increasing solar activity on the Sun's total and open magnetic flux during multiple cycles: Implications for solar forcing of climate". Geophysical Research Letters. ***29*** (24): 2224.

Lerner, K. Lee; Lerner, K. Lee; Wilmoth, Brenda (26 July 2006). Environmental issues: essential primary sources. Thomson Gale.

McGranahan, G., Balk, D., and Anderson, B. (2007) "The Rising Tide: Assessing the Risks of Climate Change and Human Settlements in Low Elevation Costal Zones", Environment and Urbanization, 19 (1), 17-37.

McKibben, Bill (2011). *The Global Warming Reader*. OR Books.

Muscheler, R; Joos, F; Müller, SA; Snowball, I (28 July 2005). "Climate: How unusual is today's solar activity?" Nature. ***436*** (7012): 1084–1087.

Oerlemans, J. (29 April 2005). "Extracting a Climate Signal from 169 Glacier Records". Science. ***308*** (5722): 675–677.

Purse, BV; Mellor, PS; Rogers, DJ; Samuel, AR; Mertens, PP; Baylis, M (February 2005). "Climate change and the recent emergence of bluetongue in Europe". Nature Reviews Microbiology. ***3*** (2): 171–181.

Revkin, Andrew C (5 November 2005). "Rise in Gases Unmatched by a History in Ancient Ice". The New York Times.

Royal Society (2005). *"Joint science academies' statement: Global response to climate change".*

Roulstone, Ian; Norbury, John (2013). *Invisible in the Storm: the role of mathematics in understanding weather.* Princeton University Press.

Ruddiman, William F. (15 December 2005). *Earth's Climate Past and Future.* New York: Princeton University Press.

Ruddiman, William F. (1 August 2005). Plows, Plagues, and Petroleum: How Humans Took Control of Climate. New Jersey: Princeton University Press.

Santer, Benjamin D.; Solomon, Susan; Wentz, Frank J.; Fu, Qiang; Po-Chedley, Stephen; Mears, Carl; Painter, Jeffrey F.; Bonfils, Céline (24 May 2017). *"Tropospheric Warming Over The Past Two Decades". Scientific Reports. 7* (2336).

Schelling, Thomas C. (2002). "Greenhouse Effect". In David R. Henderson (ed.). *Concise Encyclopedia of Economics* (1st ed.). *Library of Economics and Liberty.*

Solanki, SK; Usoskin, IG; Kromer, B; Schüssler, M; Beer, J (23 October 2004). "Unusual activity of the Sun during recent decades compared to the previous 11,000 years". Nature. ***431***(7012): 1084–1087.

Solanki, Sami K.; et al. (28 July 2005). *"Climate: How unusual is today's solar activity? (Reply)"* (PDF). Nature. ***436*** (7050): E4–E5.

Solomon, S., D. Qin, M. Manning, Z. Chen, M. Marquis, K.B. Averyt, M. Tignor, and H.L. Miller (eds.), Climate Change 2007: Impacts, Adaptation and Vulnerability, Contribution of Working Group II to the Fourth Assessment Report of the Intergovernmental Panel on Climate Change. 2007, Cambridge, United Kingdom, and New York, New York: Cambridge University Press.

Sowers, Todd (10 February 2006). "Late Quaternary Atmospheric CH_4 Isotope Record Suggests Marine Clathrates Are Stable". Science. ***311*** (5762): 838–840.

Svensmark, Henrik; et al. (8 February 2007). Experimental evidence for the role of ions in particle nucleation under atmospheric conditions. Proceedings of the Royal Society. Early Online Publishing. ***463*** (2078): 385–396.

United Nations Environment Programme, Division of Early Warning and Assessment. (2006). Emerging Challenges: New Findings, in P. Harrison (Ed.), Global Environment Outlook Year Book 2006 (59-70). Malta: Progress Press Ltd.

Walter, KM; Zimov, SA; *Chanton, JP*; Verbyla, D; Chapin, F. S., 3rd (7 September 2006). "Methane bubbling from Siberian thaw lakes as a positive feedback to climate warming". Nature. ***443*** (7107): 71–75.

Wang, Y.-M.; Lean, J.L.; Sheeley, N. R. (20 May 2005). "Modeling the sun's magnetic field and irradiance since 1713". Astrophysical Journal. ***625*** (1): 522–538.

Wiens, John J. (8 December 2016). "Climate-Related Local Extinctions Are Already Widespread among Plant and Animal Species". *PLOS Biology*. ***14*** (12.